OWNING A HORSE

Diana Gregory

OWNING
A
HORSE

A Practical Guide

Drawings by Claudia Gregory

HARPER & ROW, PUBLISHERS

New York, Hagerstown, San Francisco, London

FIRST EDITION

Designed by Stephanie Krasnow

Library of Congress Cataloging in Publication Data

Gregory, Diana.
  Owning a horse: a practical guide.
  Includes index.
  1. Horses. I. Title.
SF285.3.G73   636.1   76–9192
ISBN 0–06–011622–6

77 78 79 80 10 9 8 7 6 5 4 3 2 1

To

*My mother, who is terrified
of horses*

and

*My father, who bought me my
first horse against her
wishes*

Contents

Foreword

THIS BOOK is for the beginning horseman, especially the very young and the young at heart, for whom the Jack Benny class —a class described in this book—now becoming popular in West Coast shows, was designed. It is especially for those whose love for a horse is greater than their pocketbooks.

Ms. Gregory not only answers all the questions you've wanted to ask and were embarrassed about asking, she answers the questions you should have asked and failed to do so because of pure ignorance.

Her book prevents the heartaches caused by showing a horse costing a few hundred dollars (or raised in the owner's back yard) against the ones costing many thousands. And it opens the door to barrels of fun at little horse shows. The information ranges from an explanation of the horse's perception of radiation to instruction for making feed racks.

The book is a guide to safety, economy and pleasure with horses. Diana Gregory sits down with you and shares her experiences as a novice and her feeling about the horse world. She gives her method of saving money by making her own show and hunt attire, as well as a myriad of accessories for horse and rider. Her words about feeding, showing, trailering, stabling and many other matters, if heeded, will save the beginner disappointments, dollars and, perhaps, serious accidents.

The entire book is written with an eye on the pocketbook of the horse owner. Reading Chapter 3 may save the owner of a back-yard horse hundreds of dollars a year in veterinary bills, and might even save the horse's life.

Not only is Ms. Gregory's work delightful reading; it is also a handbook to which the wise horseman will frequently refer.

Louis Taylor

OWNING A HORSE

1

Buying, Selling, and Supporting Your Habit

MONEY. . . . Money and horses seem to go together, and more money is tossed down the drain each year by horse owners and prospective horse owners than can be counted. Paying for an overpriced horse, selling at a loss, making the wrong choice of tack or buying tack you did not need because someone told you you did, buying potions and horse cosmetics because the advertisements showing pretty horses said you needed them, needless vet bills, excessive shoeing bills—they're all there waiting to trap the unwary horse enthusiast.

Entering the world of horse ownership is somewhat similar to joining a secret cult, but no one is really sure of the right password. Even people who have owned and ridden horses for years are sometimes still operating under myths they learned from people they thought knew everything.

I hope this book will help to dispel some of those myths and some of the misinformation.

BUYING A HORSE

One important fact to keep in mind is that *it is always a buyer's market*. There is no other commodity quite like the horse. There is never a scarcity of them. This makes the selling price nearly always flexible. Bargaining is part of the buying and selling game no matter what the state of the nation's economy, or the seller's or the buyer's.

When to Buy

Horses are, because of their very nature, seasonal. In most areas of the country everyone wants to ride in the summer; consequently the peak buying time is in the spring. More pleasure horses are sold in April and May than any other months of the year. This tends to shoot the price upward as high as 40 percent during those months. Too, the horse usually looks his best then. He will have lost his rough winter coat, or have been clipped, and will have a fat, sleek appearance from a winter of grazing or stuffing himself in his stall.

If you know that you will definitely want a horse for the summer season, the best time to buy would be in February or March. The owner will have just about had it with the feed bill and should be a fairly soft sell. You can also see the horse at his worst and not be surprised next fall when you suddenly encounter a woolly mammoth in your pasture. And the owner will have forgotten just how gorgeous his steed can be.

The other best time to buy is at the end of the summer, when some owners have decided that horse ownership is not for them and will sell at a loss merely to keep from having to carry the horse through the winter months. Buy the horse, put him in winter pasture for very little money, and you will have beat the high cost of buying in the spring.

Also this is an excellent time to pick up one of the best-trained and best-cared-for horses in the world: one owned by a student just heading off to college. In most instances these horses have been owned for more than one season, have had a lot of loving care and training put into them, and

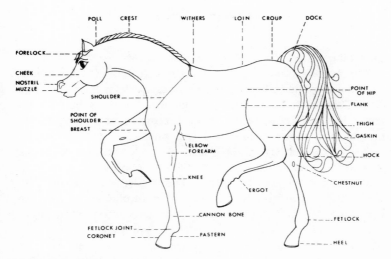

Parts of the horse.

have, most likely, been shown to some extent, so that you can tell beforehand what kind of a show career they will have with you. If you have a chance at one of these horses, you need only promise to love and cherish him and you will have obtained a real bargain no matter what price range you are looking in.

But, if you cannot contain yourself and are one of the many that decide you must buy your horse *now,* and now is April or May, at least remember that it is still a buyer's market and do not be swayed by anyone telling you, "This horse is the buy of a lifetime and will be gone tomorrow." Don't you believe it! There is always another.

Where to Buy

In the purchase of a horse, it is not so much sizing-up the horse as sizing-up the seller. Some markets are best left alone by the first-, or even the second-time buyer.

The traditional outlets are the auction, the horse trader,

the riding stable, the breeder, and the private owner.

The Auction is for the professional who has the experience to know what he is looking for and how to spot it in the sales ring. Even then he is taking a gamble. Auctions can be divided into two categories, those for grade or nonregistered horses, and those established and held for specific breeds. The *grade auction* is comprised of stock that has, for some reason or another, been unsalable in other ways. One primary point to remember is that almost anything goes and no consignor is pledged to honesty. Uncontrollable horses are frequently tranquilized, lame horses have often been given shots to relieve them temporarily of their pain so that they appear sound, and horses with obvious unsoundness, such as spavins and curbs, are kept moving at a rapid pace about the ring so that the observer is not allowed to spot such defects. And many animals that appear to be well trained, and are being shown under saddle to prove they are, have been worked for the week or so prior to the sale in just such a tight space and with such heavy-handed ways that by the time the sale rolls around they have become accustomed to working in the ring, and their mouths are so sore that they appear ready for the show circuit. After a week at home this instant training disappears. They revert to their former selves, complete with vices, and are unfit to ride. True, there are exceptions, but those belong primarily in books of juvenile fiction.

Purebred auctions are usually sponsored by a breed organization and are hence run on a higher standard. Nevertheless, the individual seller is not above stretching the truth about his particular consignment, and it takes a practiced eye to choose the right horse in the time it takes the auctioneer to run up a bid. You do have some advantage in that catalogs are usually available beforehand, listing the breeding and performance of the horses, and most of the better auctions devote the morning before the sale to giving the buyer time to examine the horses and even observe them work out in a ring if trained. It is a professional that will be handling them, however, and you will not have a chance to try yourself. And keep in mind that for the most part it is the larger breeder's excess breeding and untrained stock that will be sold at these affairs.

Horse Traders got their reputation for one reason. They earned it! The least-reputable ones are similar to used-car salesmen in that their main concern is to keep their stock moving and to make a profit. This is the marketplace of the cheap urban horse. In fact, much of their merchandise has probably been picked up at the nonbreed auctions, clipped, given a bath, shod, and shown to you as a "one-owner horse from Pasadena." *Caveat emptor* is the phrase that applies here.

The Riding Stable is a fairly safe place to buy a pleasure horse for yourself, depending upon the reputation of the establishment. The only rub here is that you are going to be paying top dollar in order to cover a built-in commission on the part of the riding stable. And, most likely, what you are going to be buying is a horse that some owner has tired of trying to sell himself and has commissioned the stable to sell for him. Avoid this middleman and do your own shopping.

The Breeder is one of the safest markets from which to buy. It is word-of-mouth and a good reputation that keep him in business. If you have plenty of money to spend and want a horse you know is going to do well in the show ring, definitely consider making a visit to a breeding farm of good reputation. Keep in mind that, for the most part, the breeder will have only young horses for sale, and therefore you will have to ante up for a rather hefty bill for professional training before your horse is ready for you. After all, if you are going to spend that kind of money for a horse, you are going to want to have him "finished" professionally. Anything else simply does not make sense. And that is a different price bracket altogether.

Private Owners are the ones you are going to be dealing with if you want to come out on top moneywise. But, a word of caution, private owners can be just as dishonest as anyone else. If you feel that something is amiss, make a hasty exit. There is always a better buy down the block.

What to Look For

Hundreds of articles and books have been written on how to choose a horse. If you have read to any appreciable extent you are now so armed with knowledge that when you do go out to buy a horse and find he does not fit neatly into all the categories that go into making up the perfect horse (and he won't), you will come away not buying. Worse yet, you might give up and buy because the owner has done a good job of selling on you.

Organize your thinking before you go out to buy, not after you have become excited over an ad in the Sunday paper extolling the virtues of some paragon of horse pulchritude.

Most important is to ask yourself, What am I looking for? If you are the average pleasure-horse buyer, what you want is a horse that will give you a smooth ride, won't cost you a fortune in vet bills, does not bring forth fits of laughter from bystanders, and has the intelligence not to walk off the nearest cliff. And if you are the average owner, even though you have no intention now of ever entering a show, just wait. So *don't overlook the possibility you might be showing that horse.* Four or five months from now, just when you and your new-found friend are perking along nicely and really getting to know one another, is not the time to discover he is not show-worthy.

It might be a good idea to list on a piece of paper what is most important to you and what least important and all the other amenities in between. You will then go out armed with something concrete and be able to say "No" to a flashy Thoroughbred gelding when what you really want is a small, grade mare for riding Western.

Now, let us take those points one at a time and you decide which is most important to you.

Type

This does not necessarily mean breed, although it can. If you are definitely looking for one particular breed, type is not a problem for you, merely money. Otherwise there are basically two types.

If you are seeking a horse to ride Western, want to participate in such activities as endurance rides and gymkhanas, and live in the Western part of the United States, the type of horse you want is smallish to medium in height and fairly stocky in build. The Quarter Horse, Morgan, Mustang, and their mixtures fall into this category. Tennessee Walkers are picking up in popularity for Western pleasure and endurance rides. Taken out of the show ring and given a chance, they are admirable horses on the trail and exceptional rides. The Arab, though of slender build, has excellent staying powers and is a popular, though very expensive, Western horse.

If what you want is a horse to show in English pleasure or hunt classes, or for just hacking along the bridle paths of your favorite park, you will be looking for a horse of slender build and a little more refinement. The height you will want depends upon your preference, the breeding of the horse, and the use he will be put to. Included in this group would be the Thoroughbred, the park-type Morgan, Arab, Tennessee Walker, and Saddlebred.

Color

Color costs money. Color does not make the horse go any better, nor does it give him a gentle disposition or intelligence. I would say that color should be at the bottom of the list, but if you have always dreamed of owning another Trigger or Black Beauty, you are going to have to pay the price. It is an interesting fact that a horse with the worst possible conformation can command a hefty price if he has a pretty enough color. There is always someone willing to pay the tariff.

Breeding

Someone once rather wisely said, "Registration papers never harmed a good horse and they never helped a poor one." There are three good reasons for owning a registered horse.

One: If you plan to breed that horse. And if you are the average horse owner, *don't.* Having a foal of your own might sound like a charming idea, but it usually results in a lot of headaches you are not prepared to take on, mostly monetary.

Two: You plan to show your horse in breed shows. Here, remember, you will be competing against the best, and if you are to win you must buy the best. Again it means money—lots of it.

Three: You can usually command a higher selling price for a registered horse. And you probably paid that price too!

If you are looking to impress your neighbors, you are better off buying a grade horse of better quality than one of registered merit with substandard looks. You can't hang those registration papers around his neck. And if you must brag about your horse, as most owners do, don't do it about his registration.

As for showing, unless you are attending shows for your specific breed, you will find that the average show has only a small percentage of classes where breed or registration counts.

The English horse is typically tall and slender; the Western horse is usually short and stocky.

Age

Now we've come to one of those myths. You have, no doubt, read or heard that the best age for purchasing a horse is between six and nine. That anything younger is immature and not settled and anything older already has one foot in horse heaven. As for maturity and reliability, some horses never do grow up mentally while others seem to be born mature. As for stamina, some competitive jumpers—and that is a hard life—are still going strong at twenty.

So forget age when you are examining your prospective

purchase. And don't bother to ask the owner. Most owners either don't really know themselves or will shave a year or five off the actual age anyway. As for wisely peering at his teeth, don't risk being bitten. Most nonprofessional people have a hard time telling age in this manner; so much depends on what the horse has been doing with those teeth in the way of eating and other habits—such as biting! Consider, instead, the other points—disposition, general appearance, health, and spirit.

If he is registered, you might take a look at the foaling date on the papers if it really matters all that much to you.

Size

Myth again. Most people equate size in a horse with strength. Some even tend to think the bigger the horse the more prestige. Well, horses have more strength than the average horseman gives them credit for, and actually it is the length of back and muscling rather than height that determines how much weight they can carry or how soon they will tire or break down.

A short man or woman should not be handicapped with a tall horse. Think of all the things you are going to be doing on the ground. You will have to saddle and bridle that horse as well as groom him, not to mention having to get on and off him. A good test is to see whether or not you can mount and dismount easily and also where your legs come in relation to using your leg aids. In other words, if you are five feet two you are going to look pretty silly mounted on a horse that is seventeen hands tall, no matter how dashing he is.

Sex

Presupposing that you are not looking for breeding material, sex then becomes a matter of personal preference and price.

Stallions are, of course, out. They are only good for breeding and running races at Churchill Downs.

That leaves you with two choices and it should be easy to make a decision, but is it?

There is that "old horseman's saying" regarding the differences in temperament between mares and geldings. The reasoning here is that mares are more unpredictable when they are in heat, which is once a month. Ask any owner of a mare when the mare was last in heat and nine out of ten won't even know. Most people have a difficult time telling when they come in at all. If, however, they have a bad day with that mare they will sagely blame it on her being in heat. After all, it's as good an excuse as any. Thus another myth is kept alive.

Then again, for reasons that no one really understands, in some parts of the country, and in some breeds, the price of one sex will be as high as 30 percent over the other. If this is the case, definitely find out which goes for less money and plan to look for that sex, and don't listen to the seller telling you how much better a gelding is or a mare is. After all he is out to make a dollar and you are out to save one.

Disposition

Temperament is paramount in a horse and should top any list. Sadly it seems to be the one amenity that the average buyer asks about last. It goes without saying that you are not going to buy a horse with obvious bad vices, such as kicking or biting, but what about some of those minor vices that you might forget to check on, yet that take on tremendous proportions when you get him home?

Is he hard to catch in a pasture? Does he act nervous when you walk around him? Does he resist having his feet picked up? Does he stand still when you mount him or does he try to walk nervously off? Does he shy easily? Does he feel like a bundle of nerves when you are astride him? And

—one important vice often overlooked until it is too late— how well does he ride in a trailer? You can disregard one or two of these minor vices, but any more will tend to take away from the pleasure of riding, and isn't that what you are after, a pleasure horse?

Training

This is one area in which you cannot be thrifty if what you want is a professionally trained, "push-button" horse ready for the show arena. It takes a good six months to get a horse to this stage. At an average of $200 to $350 per month for professional training you can figure what the final bill will be.

On the other hand, if you check some of the horses owned by youngsters who have been showing and have done much of the training themselves, you just may find a horse that almost equals one from a professional stable and that has spent at least one season in the show circuit. The cost of these horses will be about half that of a professionally trained mount yet to be tried in the ring. Please keep in mind we are not talking about national show mounts. That is a different group altogether and one usually composed of millionaires.

Conformation

In body structure the key words to consider are *locomotion* and *balance.* The idea is to have a smooth ride and own a horse that is not going to fall apart at the seams because he is put together badly.

When purchasing your first horse do not try to learn all the finer points of anatomy. That will come in time. You should not be planning to put your life savings into your first horse anyway, hence you will get by nicely by paying attention to only a few key areas. If most of these line up, more than likely the rest of the horse is going to line up as well.

The Head Do you like it? Does the horse appear intelligent? Are his ears of reasonable size and alert? Not nervous . . . *alert.* Are his eyes large and soft, wide apart, and fairly low on his head, or are they small and piglike? His nose should be either straight or dished, not bowed out unbecomingly. And his jaws should be deep and well formed.

The Neck This is more than a mere attachment for the head. It helps the horse to maintain his balance. Fifty percent of the horse should be in front of the withers and fifty percent behind them. It doesn't take much imagination to draw

Fifty percent of the body should be in front of the withers and 50 percent behind.

a line mentally at the point of the withers and check this percentage. Look to see if the head joins the neck at right angles and if the neckline is relatively straight.

The Topline This includes those withers again. Are they prominent enough to keep the saddle from slipping forward when going downhill? Does the back cave in? This denotes weakness. Don't worry about the rump. Rumps are rumps and everyone likes something different.

The Shoulder Smoothness of ride is related to the angle of the shoulder. It should slope at an *angle* rather than be straight up and down. If you can't readily see the angle, lay your arm along the shoulder where it joins the neck. It should then be fairly obvious to you.

Good conformation is a matter of the right angles being in the right places. Try to match these angles when looking for a horse to buy.

The Legs These are your locomotion. Forget all those complicated instructions about judging legs. There are two key points: the *cannon* bone, between the knee and hock and the ankle; and the *pastern,* between the ankle and the hoof. The cannon bone should be relatively short. It should be wide and flat when viewed from the side and straight from knee and hock to ankle and flow smoothly into those bones. When a horse has passed this test, he is said to have "good bone." The pastern is the shock absorber, and it should be fairly long and angular, not short and straight up and down.

Leg Injuries You have, no doubt, read or been warned about such as ring bone, side bone, splints, spavins, bowed tendons, and the like. Some of the obvious ones, such as splints, can look fairly horrible but in reality aren't, so long as they are not located close to a joint; while others such as ring and side bone cannot always be detected. If the leg looks clean to you, fine. *Let the vet give the final O.K.* (You *are,* one hopes, going to have a vet check before you buy!) Do take a look at the feet for abnormal ridges and other signs of founder, but don't worry excessively over cracks and dryness.

Now stand back and take an overall look at the horse. Does he look strong and hardy? This is termed "substance." Does he give you a feeling of nobility or fineness? This is termed "quality." Give him ten extra points if he possesses either of these characteristics.

THE BUYING TRIP

You have written the items on your list in order of importance to you. You have then located a prospective horse and have made an appointment. Now, plan your trip. *Arrive half an hour early . . .* apologize, but arrive early. This will achieve two things for your side. One: it will put the seller off just enough so that you will have the early advantage. Two: he will probably not have had the chance to get the horse "ready" for you and you can observe his manners as he is being caught or led out of his stall.

Try to make your first observation of the horse from a distance, at least fifteen feet, and take a look at the overall picture. Note those points mentioned under conformation. A quick glance should tell you if he is all there.

Next, ask the owner to saddle and ride the horse. *Don't ride the horse yourself first!* You can tell more about the horse's action and way of going from a ground viewpoint than you can by riding him and worrying about how *you* are doing. Ask the owner to ride at a trot as well as a canter, or lope, and to take both leads. Note any deviation from normal leg movement, such as excessive toeing in or out or one leg interfering with another. Finally, have the owner back the horse. This is important. Would you buy a car that didn't have a reverse gear?

If you still like what you see, ride him yourself and follow the same procedure. Try to ride him both in the ring, if there is one, and on the trail.

If he is registered, ask to see his papers. Not that you are going to gain any great information by doing so, but you do want to know that they are available and not "lost."

Ask the owner if he objects to your having a vet check the horse to make sure he is in good health and sound. No one that is honest should object to this. If the owner says he is in a hurry to sell and needs the money today, or some such excuse, say good-bye and leave, no matter how much you have fallen for that horse. If he doesn't object, tell him you like the horse very much but you do have one other to look at and will call him the next day. *Do not discuss price* other than to ask how much.

Next is the most important step: *Go home and sleep on it!* If you are unable to sleep, that is the horse for you. Now is when you do your bargaining. Call the owner and tell him you would like to buy the horse but that the price is just a little more than you can afford. Then offer him a definite, and fair, amount to consider. Should he accept your price, great! Go right out and give him a check with the provision that it be held until the horse passes the vet check. (You might postdate the check.) Should he decline to drop the price and you still want the horse, at least you have tried. Perhaps he has just put the horse on the market and isn't all that anxious yet. If you want to give it a further try, wait a week and contact him again.

Call your vet and set up an appointment as soon as possible in consideration of the owner. Important: *Be there when the vet comes.* This is the time to ask any questions you are not clear on and to ask the owner about what shots the horse has had and what worming schedule he has followed. The owner won't fib about this in front of the vet.

As for money, the cost of the vet check is the best $10 to $25 you will ever invest. *Don't skip this step.*

One point of contention that can truly be touchy if it is not handled properly at the time of the sale is the registration. The proper transfer should be handled at the time of the sale. If for some reason, and it can be real, he does not have a transfer slip, etc., offer to pay him half the amount now and the balance when the paper is delivered to you.

Do pay by check if you can, writing "Paid in full" on the face of the check. You will not only have proof of purchase but you will have a little time in case there is something amiss when you get him home: you can always stop payment. By "amiss" I don't mean a trailering accident that is your fault; I mean something really wrong that was not noticeable until you got him on home ground.

Be sure to get a proper bill of sale as well, one with the description of the horse, the amount you paid, and the date, and *keep it.* The selling of stolen horses is a popular pastime in some areas of the country. So is selling a horse and then reporting it missing.

That's it. Take him home and enjoy him . . . knowing that you made a good deal.

SELLING AT A PROFIT

By now you should understand what is involved in determining the asking price and the selling price of a horse and how to work it in your favor. You should understand that emotion plays a great part in the buying and selling of horses and work on that principle. At least 50 percent of the time horses are sold because of emotion: you've chased him around that pasture for the last time . . . there's another horse you want so badly you could cry . . . or you've paid your last feed bill and that's that. *Hold on.* Those are not reasons for selling at a loss. The only reason for selling at a loss is that you have been suddenly transferred to Iraq and you have to leave tomorrow. Even then there are ways.

When to Sell

You know when the best time is—those early months in spring. But what if your timing is not perfect and when you decide to sell it is midsummer, or worse yet, midwinter? If it is midsummer you are still in luck. If you are showing your steed, terrific! Continue to take him to shows and put him in only the classes he really does well in. If you check with the announcer prior to the beginning of the class, he will most likely be happy to mention that "The horse that just placed third in this class is for sale. See the owner if you are interested." There you are . . . the best free advertising in the world. And that's the name of the game. Try to avoid paying for advertising whenever possible. Your margin is not so big that you can afford to run up a large bill at the local newspaper office. Sometimes it can't be helped, but exhaust other ways first.

Spend an evening and make up some attractive five-by-eight cards advertising him for sale. Be specific. Stress the salable points, such as registration or training or color. Add his picture if you have a flattering one. Then spend an afternoon putting them on bulletin boards at all the local tack shops and riding schools, and on any other bulletin boards that are in your neighborhood.

Let those riding stables work in your behalf. Set a definite price and see if they would be interested in working on a commission above that.

If it is midwinter, *don't sell,* no matter how much you are tempted. In any section of the country there are places where you can winter pasture your horse for a very small fee. This will get the horse out of your sight, as well as nice and fat and rested and ready to sell in those spring months. Wait until March and bring him home and spiff him up.

Making the Best of Him

If you've ever sold a car or a house, you have the general idea. Make him look "brand new."

Start grooming him daily to get his coat and general condition up. Blanket him at night to get his coat lying smooth. Add some flax seed, or other inexpensive coat conditioner, to his grain. Worm him. Worms make a coat dull no matter how much conditioner you are pouring into him.

Have him shod. Don't wait until the last minute for this either. His feet could be tender, and who needs a horse that appears to be permanently crippled?

Begin riding him at least two or three times a week if you can and the weather permits. It is nearly impossible to show a horse well that hasn't been regularly ridden for a few weeks. (But perhaps the reason you want to sell him is that he has developed some habits or had an about-face in the personality department and you are terrified of him. In that case check your local newspaper for small-time trainers, call one, and make a deal to have him take the horse, work him out, and sell him. Split the profit and drown your sorrows in a good stiff drink. No amount of money is worth a broken neck.)

Get out any tack that you plan to use to sell him and polish it as if you were going to a show. Keep his stall or other quarters neat and tidy. It is subliminal but it gets the message across.

And, speaking of tack, *don't offer tack for sale with the horse!* They are not a set. Offering tack and horse together puts your horse into the cheap back-yard classification and tells your buyer in letters three feet high you "just want out" and will probably take the first price he offers.

Tack is something you can take your time selling. It doesn't eat nor does it take up much space. Wait until after your horse is sold. It is even possible that your buyer may offer to purchase the tack along with the horse, especially after you have put so much effort into cleaning and polishing.

If you don't want to bother selling the tack yourself, take it to a riding shop. They'll be happy to sell it on consignment for you.

SUPPORTING YOUR HABIT

If you are the average horse owner, you are not overly burdened with money and those bills can sneak up on you pretty fast. There *is* something you can do about it. It doesn't matter if you are nine or ninety, work, attend school, or slave at home with ten children. If you have time for a horse, you have time to make the money to support it. Try some of these ideas.

Selling Manure If you have a pickup, offer to deliver it for so much a load. If not, sell it by the sackful. Use the empty feed sacks for packaging—sort of a recycling process. Not only does this bring in money, it gets rid of the flies.

Boarding
Riding
Lessons
Manure for Sale

Paint Fences If you live in an area that abounds in pastures with fences, take a look at some of those that are in dire need of painting and offer to paint them. After all, it *is* horse-related and you should not feel as though you are merely doing manual labor. Stop every once in a while and admire the horses in the field.

Clean Stalls People who work do not look forward to doing this chore on weekends. If you are a housewife, student, or other stay-at-home worker, offer a service and spend a couple of mornings a week doing this. It's more fun than housework and burns up calories besides.

Exercising Other People's Horses It is surprising how many people buy horses, install them in their homes, and then ride only once a month or so. They usually feel guilty about this and that is where you come in.

Grooming Many people who work all week yet want to show on Saturday just do not have the time to get their horses ready. If you are free, try operating a Friday grooming service. This could include braiding manes and tails, clipping legs and heads, and, if the horse is really dirty, bathing.

Braiding Manes and Tails Some people never do learn this art and will gladly pay to have it done. Go early to shows and offer your services.

Teach Riding You must have some proficiency, but if you've been riding for two or more years, you could offer beginners' lessons to youngsters around the neighborhood. Don't forget to check your insurance policy before you do, however, to be sure you are covered against anyone's being injured on your property. You might also post a sign saying, "Anyone riding does so at his own risk." Most establishments do this. Although it won't really protect you from a damage suit, it does serve as a legal warning.

Boarding Should you have a couple of acres going to waste, or an extra stall, this is the perfect answer. Have the horse owners sign agreements that absolve you of any injuries that might occur either to them or the horses and make sure you have the right to call a vet in case of emergency, with bills going to them. You might also state that you will lock up their horses if board is not paid and even sell them for costs after so much time. Give them a copy of the agreement and keep one on file. (Friendships pale when things are not in writing.)

Offer Lay-ups This is basically the same as boarding except that you only take the horse in for a short period of time —like a motel for horses. This has one advantage over boarding in that you are not always tied down and can keep the lay-ups to periods that are convenient to you.

Make Horse Objects Try making and selling any one of the easily made objects in Chapter 7. These can include fly masks, woven saddle blankets, custom-fitted stable blankets, tack boxes, saddle racks, jumps, saddle covers, or even show apparel (see Chapter 9).

Take Photos If you are a photo nut, try setting up a business at the local shows. You can offer to take pictures of the winners and even nonwinners.

Paint Portraits If your hobby is painting, why not try horses? Animal portraits make great Christmas presents, and what better way to spend the winter evenings? Make a sample by painting your own horse and ask to hang it in the local tack shop. Leave a pile of business cards with them and you are on your way to a mild fortune.

Write Try your hand at writing articles, fillers, and puzzles for horse magazines.

And don't spend all your income on advertising. Use those

five-by-eight cards in the right places, and if you need them, you can get some inexpensive business cards made up for less than $10.

Whatever you find to do to help pay the costs of horse ownership, it will probably result in the meeting of new horse friends, and that can be a terrific plus!

HORSE TALK

Aged   Used to describe a horse ten (some people say nine) years old and older.

Aids   The legs, hands, and weight as they are used to control the horse.

Colors of horses

Black   True black without light areas; black mane and tail.

Brown   Often mistaken for black; however, the flanks and muzzle are brown.

Bay   Ranging from tan, through red, to reddish brown color with black points (lower legs), mane, and tail.

Blood bay   Reddish brown with black points, mane, and tail.

Sandy bay   Light brown with black points, mane, and tail.

Chestnut   Dark reddish-brown with either matching mane and tail or flaxen mane and tail.

Liver chestnut   Includes all dark chestnut colors but especially that shade which is the same as a piece of raw liver. May have mane and tail same color as body or flaxen.

Sorrel   Light reddish-brown or copper color with mane and tail matching or flaxen.

Palomino   Golden yellow with white mane and tail.

Dun   Yellow with black mane and tail and black dorsal stripe.

Buckskin   Yellow-gray with black mane and tail and black dorsal stripe.

Red dun   Dun color with reddish mane and tail.

Grullo   Mouse color with black mane and tail, usually with black points.

Gray   Mixture of black and white hairs, usually born darker and becoming lighter with age.

Rose gray   Gray with chestnut hairs mixed in.

Red roan   Uniform mixture of red and white hairs.

Blue roan   Uniform mixture of black and white hairs usually with some red mixed in.

Piebald   Mixture of black and white areas (sometimes called a *pinto*).

Skewbald   Same as piebald except that colors are bay, chestnut and brown on white, or vice versa.

Coarse   Rough in appearance, lacking in refinement.

Colt   A young male horse.

Conformation   The build or general structure of the horse.

Dam   The female parent of a horse.

Filly   A female horse up to three years of age, at which time she becomes a mare.

Gait   The way of going. The usual gaits of the pleasure horse are walk, trot, and canter or lope.

Gelding   An altered or castrated horse.

Grade horse   An unregistered horse.

Green horse   A horse with little or no training.

Hand   A unit of four inches used to measure the height of a horse; measured from the withers to the ground.

Mare   A female horse three years old or over.

Proud cut   To describe a horse that has been improperly cut and hence acts like a stallion, yet cannot breed.

Push button   To describe a horse so well trained that he responds to almost imperceptible cues.

Quality   Fineness of conformation.

Registration   Papers showing that a horse is registered in an association with stud book and breeding record.

Sire   The male parent of a horse.

Sound   Physically fit with no signs of weakness or illness.

Substance   Strength and stamina.

Stallion   A mature male horse that is used for breeding.

Stud   The place where stallions are kept for breeding. Sometimes, incorrectly, used to describe a stallion.

Tack   Equipment used for riding, such as saddle, bridle, etc.

Vet check   A physical given by a veterinarian, usually in conjunction with the purchase of a horse.

Vice   A bad habit.

2

Feeding and Facts

ONE SURE THING you can count on—feeding your horse is going to have a drastic effect on your budget. The person who originally said, "That ain't hay," certainly wasn't discussing today's alfalfa prices.

And, if you add the cost of food supplements, coat conditioners, and the various concoctions sold in feed stores, you are soon going to wonder if horse ownership is really worth it.

What this chapter is about, then, is how to feed your horse and keep him and your budget fit.

HOW TO FEED YOUR HORSE LESS

Feed requirements are going to vary with every horse. It may require almost twice as much feed to keep a tall, nervous horse fit as it does a short, stocky, even-tempered horse of the same weight. (If you have not yet bought your horse, you might keep this fact in mind.) However, almost any horse can be made into what is termed an "easy keeper"—that is, a horse that will do well on a smaller amount of feed than another of the same weight.

That basic premise is simple and has been tested and proven several times over. Try it for a period of six or eight weeks and see if you don't notice a very real difference.

Your horse should be fed in the same place and at the same time every day (within fifteen minutes). As with Pavlov's dog, your horse's digestive juices will start to flow at a specific time, and he will be ready to utilize every little bit of protein and carbohydrate that you will be giving him. Nor will he be fretting about where he is to find his meal.

One other point to be considered is whether or not he is getting all he can out of what you are giving him.

Are his teeth up to par? Horses are strange creatures in many ways when it comes to eating. They chew on only one side at a time and this tends to turn their teeth into jagged little ridges. Your horse's teeth should be checked occasionally to see if they need floating, or grinding down, so that he has an even surface with which to work.

One way to tell if he needs some dental work is to examine his manure. If the grain that you are giving him is making the trip through unscathed, then something is certainly amiss in the mouth department. Also, if he is slobbering a great deal or dropping large mouthfuls of grain all over the place, you might suspect the same thing. Unlike people, horses don't have enzymes in their saliva to break down their food, thus their teeth must take care of this job.

There is no need to rush to the phone to call the vet, but if you are having him worm your horse you might have him do the dental work at the same time.

And while we are on the subject of wiggly things, how long has it been since your horse has been wormed? If he is stuffed to the back molars with worms it is a sure thing that he is not going to get his fair share of the vittles. Worming is taken up at length in another part of this book, but whether you do it yourself or have your vet do it, *plan a worming schedule* and stick to it.

Keep in mind some other tidbits of information that will help you keep your steed fit on a smaller amount of food. These relate to his digestive system.

Your horse's stomach is quite small by comparison to ours, and that old bromide about eating like a horse simply does not apply. The horse is a grazing animal and his internal workings are set up to accommodate him for this. The food does not remain in one place but is always moving. Food retention averages one and a half hours. The digestion and ingestion in the small intestine are much more important than what occurs in the stomach. Therefore, the more often you feed your horse, the closer you are coming to nature's plan, and the more food is going to be utilized. If you are a homebody you might consider a feeding schedule of three or four times a day rather than the standard morning and evening. Horses like to nibble at night and a 10 P.M. feeding might just be the ticket to a sleeker appearance and a lighter budget.

Plan to allow your horse plenty of time to digest his meals before you take him out for a romp. His body needs to concentrate its blood supply on those internal workings, not on running down the trail. And, of course, to work any horse immediately after he has eaten is to invite such costly happenings as colic and similar digestive upsets.

It takes approximately ten to fifteen minutes for him to eat a pound of hay and about five to ten minutes to consume a pound of grain. Calculate how long it will take him to gobble down his meal, add about an hour, and then plan on saddling up. But, if your usual hour to ride is 5 A.M., for goodness sake don't get up and feed him at 3 A.M. Give him breakfast when you get home. I think he would prefer that.

WHAT HE REALLY NEEDS

If you have unlimited monetary resources and you want to put a full gourmet meal on the table for your pet, more power to you. But if you are working hard just to try to support him, realize that it can be done without harm to his physical well-being in several ways. Pasture is one of the ways.

The cost of a good pasture is approximately one-half that of hay, yet a *good* pasture will supply your horse with all the nutrients he needs for his own maintenance plus an hour or two of work for you.

If you are boarding your horse out, you might consider pas-

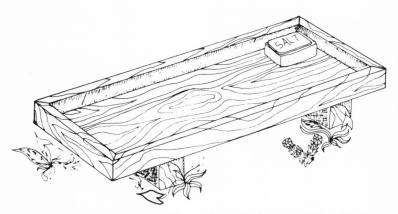

The pasture horse needs something to keep his hay out of the dirt. This simple feeder is easy to make. The directions are in Chapter 7.

ture boarding over the conventional boarding stable. In our part of the country this can be done for as little as ten dollars a month. If you have one or two acres of your own you might even consider putting in one yourself. You need not have a degree in agriculture or even a green thumb to make it thrive.

Unless you have adobe or hard-pan soil that is like a concrete runway, you probably won't even need to do anything as drastic as plowing, disking, or anything else remotely resembling a farm activity.

Your first project will be to take a sample of the soil to a nearby agricultural college or county agricultural agent, and have it tested—usually free. Or check with your farm advisor as to where it can be sent—usually free, also. When the analysis comes back, read enough to find out what your soil requires. If you are lucky and your soil is eager to grow almost anything, take a trip to your feed dealer, who will then supply you with the right mixture of seed for your area. (Of course, if you live in snow country, you realize that you are going to have to wait until spring for this activity.) Go home and scatter the seed by hand—so many pounds to the acre, just as the feed dealer recommends. Water it well and keep it going by frequent watering.

Should you be so fortunate as to be able to put in underground sprinklers, this is going to save you a lot of work. Be sure to put old tires or something similar around the sprinkler heads to protect them from the horse and the horse from them. If, however, you are not so fortunate and your coffers do not run to having them installed, you might try combining several lengths of garden hose along with an oscillating sprinkler head. It works just as well.

Now let us return to those who have unfriendly soils. Should this be your problem you can solve it in one easy operation. Rent a small tractor from your nearby rental company and spend an afternoon disking up your soil. Add any nutrients or fertilizer that have been suggested on your analysis as you go along. It really doesn't take long, and requires only native intelligence and an ability to steer the tractor.

While you are sowing or disking be sure to check the field for such hazards as broken glass, rusty cans, tree stumps, pipes, and hidden holes.

It is best to split your pasture in two and let your horse graze on one side while the other is recuperating. Different pastures recuperate at different speeds, but a good rule-of-thumb is to let your horse graze it down to about two inches and then move him.

One acre should take care of one horse. Horses on good pasture year round will get all they need for their maintenance. They store up nutrients when the grazing is lush, then use the surplus when there is less grass.

If you have less than one acre to devote to pasture, you will still be ahead of the game if you divide your horse's living quarters into two separate areas and put in a small pasture on one side, even if it is no bigger than a quarter of an acre. Use it to let him graze one or two hours a day.

When first putting your horse out on pasture, do so gradually, starting with twenty minutes the first day and increasing it over a period of two or three weeks to prevent any digestive upsets. Do not fret if your horse has rather loose bowels at first. This is normal. He will soon become used to the change. Any way you look at it, pastures no matter what their size are great. They put your horse in his natural habitat even if only for a short period of time.

GRASS CLIPPINGS

If you are like many suburban horse owners and your entire spread consists of a one-third-acre plot, including your split-level rancho, there are still ways to get fresh greenery inside your horse. Grass clippings are a terrific treat for someone used to a pile of dry hay. *Only ecology-approved clippings, with no bits of oleander or azalea leaves,* should be used. Do not feed him clippings from a lawn that has had pesticides, herbicides, or nonorganic fertilizers applied at any time during its growth.

Clippings can be dried also and used just like any other hay. To harvest, spread them out where the sun can dry them thoroughly—not in a pile where they will heat up and not dry properly. Fill up your empty feed sacks and feed along with your regular hay. Just remember that grass clippings must be fed fresh or dried *completely.*

HAY

For the horse not on pasture, this will be the mainstay of his diet, if not the complete diet. Many authorities will go into great lengths and detail about hay—which types are best, which cuttings are best, how long it should lie in the field before it is baled, etc. This is great. But let's face it: what you get is what you get. It all depends on where you live. I live in California. Many of the hays discussed by these authorities I have never laid eyes on. The feed stores in my neck of the woods (and California has more horses than any other state) give you a choice of two types of hay: alfalfa and oat hay. In fact in southern California 90 percent of the horses dine strictly on alfalfa. Until I was somewhere in my teens I thought "alfalfa" was a synonym for "hay." Yet many authorities stress that a diet of alfalfa alone is too rich and will only invite disastrous digestive results every time. Obviously they don't live in southern California.

So keep your steed happy and your wallet happy and don't try to find hay that isn't grown in your area. Look for the best quality of whatever is offered and hope that at least 50 percent of it is legume hay. That is the one with protein. Legumes are plants of the pea family and produce seeds in a pod. Some legumes are alfalfa, trefoil, and the various clovers. The grass hays include timothy, prairie hay, orchard grass, bromegrass (called brome), Bermuda grass, and Kentucky bluegrass.

Judging Hay

"Break open a bale and check for color and leafiness." Does that sentence sound familiar to you? In my feed store if you break open a bale, you've bought it. Oh, I suppose if you are buying by the ton you might just get away with that sort of behavior, although I have yet to see it done. Moreover, you as a one- or two-horse owner will not be buying by the ton if you follow my advice.

Buy only the amount of hay that you can use up in six to eight weeks, and that much only if you have the proper storage area. Proper storage does not mean some planks in an open field with a tarp over it. Unless you live in the Gobi Desert the rain or snow is going to attack that hay no matter what. And if you do live in the Gobi Desert you will probably end up with gritty hay, and no horse would appreciate that. The main point is that you want to serve up fairly fresh hay. If you check to see how often your feed store receives its supply, no doubt you will find that it is on a weekly schedule.

Do not buy hay that is more than six months old. One way

to tell if it has been stored somewhere else before it has reached your dealer is to take a look at the baling wire. If it looks rusty, pass it by and go someplace else.

And don't let the dealer talk you into buying a ton because it is a bit cheaper that way. If you have no storage space or won't be using it up quickly enough, that is *no bargain.*

To check the quality of hay you need only pull some of it loose from the middle of the bale. The main characteristic of all good hay is leafiness, because that is where the nourishment is—but it should not be excessively leafy; that kind is for rabbits.

Next in importance is color. If the type of hay you are looking at is supposed to be green, as is alfalfa, make sure it has most of its color left. If it is the yellow type, such as oat hay, it still should have a faint tinge of green remaining. In other words, it should not so closely resemble the straw piled next to it that it is difficult to tell the two apart.

Finally, check the stems. Ideally they should be soft and pliable, not coarse and brittle.

All hay should have a pleasant odor. If there is no odor at all, the hay is so old that most of its vitamin A content has been lost. Dusty hay is most undesirable. Not only is it unpalatable but dust particles will get into your horse's lungs, mucous membranes and eyes.

As for mold or mildew, they happen to the best of dealers. This can occur when hay has been baled wet or not allowed to cure properly. If you should run across a bale with more than its share, return it and your dealer should be happy to exchange it for you. Do not berate him. It is not his fault, just a fact of life that does occur—although should it occur too frequently take your business elsewhere.

Feeding Hay

If your horse lives in a stall, you will save money and keep your horse a lot healthier if you provide him with a manger in which to serve up his hay. Should you give him hay on the

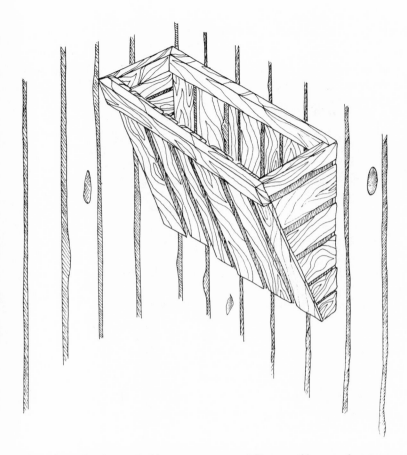

If you are planning to build a manger you might copy this one. A narrow opening at the bottom allows the old hay to fall through so that it does not accumulate.

floor he will mix a great portion of it in with his bedding or make a mistake in it when he has turned around to get a drink of water. These two actions will waste a lot of that expensive hay. If you don't have a manger you might set aside a Saturday sometime soon to make one. Anyone can do it.

Hay nets are another matter. I know they sell a lot of them but I don't approve too heartily of them. A net must be hung high enough to insure that the horse will not get a hoof caught in it should he paw at it. This means that the net will be high enough so that dust and chaff will then fall into his eyes and nostrils as he eats. They are also a pain in the neck to fill and hang.

If your horse spends his time in a corral, a large flat box that you can put together just as easily as that manger (see Chapter 7) would certainly be preferable to the ground. Ground gets muddy in the winter and dusty in the summer. Neither mud nor dust is good for your horse's stomach, and he is going to waste a lot of food by scattering it around and stomping on it.

Whether you feed him in his stall or in a corral be sure that he has a good supply of water handy, as eating hay is thirsty work, but don't have the water next to the hay supply. Horses are sloppy eaters.

Before you serve up that hay be sure to shake it out and check for any foreign objects, such as sharp rocks, pieces of wire, star thistle, or dead mice—all very disturbing to the appetite.

If you feed your horse twice a day, feed him one-third of his ration in the morning and two-thirds in the evening. Presumably you will be riding him during the day, giving him the evening hours to digest the larger portion.

CONCENTRATES

The word "concentrate" is a nice horsy term for grain. The alimentary canal of a horse is not naturally suited for the digestion of concentrates. This is a man-added nutrient. Briefly, not many horses have died of too much roughage, but a lot have died of a too hefty serving of concentrates.

Of the grains, oats are the first choice among most horsemen, being fairly high in protein and safest, owing to the bulk made by the hulls. They come in different forms: whole, crimped, and rolled. Whole oats have one advantage, in that

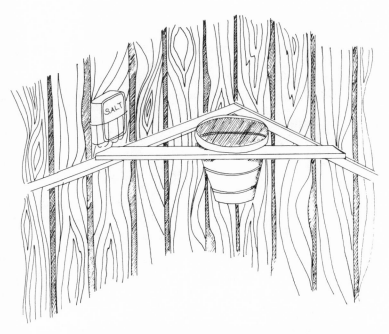

A board nailed across one corner of the stall is an easy way to keep the water bucket off the floor.

you can easily see what quality you are getting by looking for good yellow color and dry, crisp hulls. But some horses tend to bolt their grain and will not chew it enough to break down the individual grains so that digestion can occur in the stomach and lower intestines. You might, therefore, be better off buying the crimped or rolled variety.

Corn is a concentrate high in carbohydrates and as such has a great deal of fattening quality to it.

Barley by itself is not too popular a grain. It must be rolled or soaked overnight before serving. Indeed, if you check your feed store you will no doubt see that it is put in with corn and the mixture is called "barley-corn."

Bran is the one concentrate that should be in every feed room. It is the outer covering of any grain, usually wheat, and has twice the bulk of oats. It has a laxative quality and according to leading veterinarians should be included in every measure of grain you feed your horse. A good ratio is one part bran to four parts of whatever other grain you are feeding. It will keep your horse's stomach happy and you won't be calling the vet out for a horse with colic from eating too many concentrates.

Conditioners

There is a further group of concentrates that are so high in protein that they are considered "protein supplements." I classify these as coat conditioners and start adding a *small* amount about six weeks before show season starts and on through to the end. The cost is minimal when you add this amount, and you can even continue to do so all year, should you desire. Some of these are soy-oil meal, linseed-oil meal, cottonseed-oil meal and flax seed. A small handful added to the grain will do the trick. It is certainly just as effective as some of the high-cost coat conditioners pushed over the counter in various plastic containers.

Feeding Grain

Grain should always be fed in some sort of container, *never* on the ground. If your horse is to be fed out in the pasture, try to attach the feeder to the fence, or a post, instead of just leaving it loose on the ground. Most horses will put their foot in the box to keep it from moving about and consequently the box will tip over and there goes the grain onto the ground just where you don't want it.

Always change any grain ration gradually, whether it is a change in type or a change in amount, unless you are suddenly taking an active horse out of service for a while; then, of course, your change should be a sudden cutback by at least half.

Storage

Grain comes in heavy paper sacks or burlap bags. Do not leave it that way. Get yourself a good waterproof, rodent-proof, horse-proof garbage can, and transfer that feed the minute you get it home.

Measurements

Most horsemen think in terms of quarts and gallons instead of pounds. You will end confusion for yourself if you take a two-pound coffee can and print the various measurements of different grains as quarts on the side. Oats weigh one pound to the quart, barley one and a half pounds to the quart, and shelled corn one and three-quarters pounds to the quart. That way you'll never be just guessing at the proper amounts—a guessing game in which you are bound to be the loser.

FRUITS AND VEGETABLES

Your horse is going to thank you if you occasionally give him a few fresh fruits or vegetables along with his standard diet. This is not to say that you should run out and buy up a lot of expensive produce. However, should you run across a good buy or have a garden with a surplus that you don't feel like canning, his feed box is a good place to put it. You can safely give him carrots, turnips, parsnips, pumpkins, squash, peaches, pears, plums, and apples. Be sure the seeds are out of the fruit and that you cut everything up into bite-sized chunks. And remove them from his feeder if he declines to partake. Remember the word is occasionally, and these fruits and vegetables are an addition to his diet—sort of a dessert for being a good boy.

PELLETED FEEDS

I am not going to win any plaudits from the horse industry for what I am about to say, but as far as I am concerned pelleted feeds should never have been invented. To me they are like the "plastic" convenience foods you find in your supermarket. They are made by compressing the hay and other ingredients together under high heat. No one can tell me that sort of thing is good for any foodstuff. I know they say that the nutrients are all there and the roughage is just the same as it was when nature made it. That is what the food manufacturers of sugar-coated cereals keep saying, too.

One other point of contention, and a big one, is that your horse is an animal designed for almost constant eating. He can chomp down a ration of pellets in a matter of minutes. What is he supposed to do for the rest of the day? Well, you know what he does for the rest of the day! He eats his stall or your fence or the neighbors' hedge—all forbidden for his digestive system, especially if the hedge is oleander, which is rather lethal.

SUPPLEMENTS

This chapter is not meant to show you how to turn an undernourished, poorly kept horse into a healthy one. I am supposing you bought a healthy one in the first place and merely want to keep him that way.

Suppliers of supplements and feed dealers would like you to believe that *all* horses need supplements. Why not? That is how they make their money! If you will look at this in a rational light I think you can see how this thinking might be in error. Compare your horse to yourself; and remember that your horse probably eats better. If you stopped taking that

1-A-Day-With-Iron would you suddenly fall dead of nutritional disease? I really think not. Try it for about six months and see if you really can notice any difference. Good! Now I've saved you the cost of those vitamin pills as well.

Before I am attacked by the horse-business moguls, let me qualify myself. Supplements do have a place. If you have a malnourished horse, a mare in foal, a horse under one year who is busy doing 50 percent of his growing, by all means run out and plunk down that green stuff for a can of supplements. But, if not, you are better off spending that $5 to $20 on a bag of oats or what-have-you. Just as *you* don't need those vitamins if you are enjoying the benefits of a balanced day's rations, your horse doesn't need them either.

Also, do not fall for the one labeled "coat conditioner" unless you have so much loot that you don't know what to do with it all. This supplement is mostly vitamins and minerals with some natural coat conditioner added. Instead add a little more elbow grease to his hide in the way of daily grooming.

SALT

Horses *need* salt. Salt helps to maintain the correct balance of water in the horse's system and in all his cells. It stimulates digestion and it helps prevent the blood from becoming overcharged with harmful gases.

The cost of a salt block is hardly worth considering. If you keep it in a container that will protect it from the rain, a fifty-pound block should last you several months. Salt blocks come in several varieties, including plain, trace-mineral, and ones to keep the ticks away. Most folks I know like the trace-mineral one, as it insures your horse's getting any minerals that just might be missing from his feed.

Horses normally need about two ounces a day. Don't worry about your horse getting too much. A healthy horse won't eat an excessive amount unless he's actually been deprived for some time.

WATER

It is amazing how often people will neglect to check their horse's water. Perhaps a few facts will bring home the importance to you so that you will never again be guilty of this dastardly deed.

- Water forms three-quarters of the entire weight of the adult horse
- The water contained in the alimentary canal and used for digestive purposes is double what a horse consumes in a twenty-four-hour period

An old bathtub makes a sturdy and economical water trough.

- The average horse drinks about ten to twelve gallons a day, more in warm weather
- For every two and a half pounds of hay the horse eats he must produce a gallon of saliva and for the same weight in grain a quart

What we are talking about is *fresh* water. Never be content to top off a dirty pail or tub. Your horse won't like drinking it any more than you would.

Water containers needn't be elegant or expensive. In the pasture the best type is an old-fashioned bathtub. These can be acquired by contacting a house-wrecking firm, or checking the want ads. You should be able to get one for as little as $10. That's much less than the $60 or $70 you would pay for a galvanized tub at the feed dealer's. Laundry tubs are also good.

For his stall, force yourself to spend the money and buy one of those really nice hard rubber buckets. Nail a board across one corner of the stall, preferably near the door, and slip the bucket into the space. Never leave a bucket on the floor. All sorts of things will fall into it and your horse will end up kicking it around the stall. No material can withstand that kind of punishment for long.

Automatic waterers are terrific. They have them in all the best places. But the best places can usually afford them. If you can, buy one by all means. If you can't, don't fret. Buckets have been around for a lot longer.

Clean your tub or pail once a week with disinfectant. Just be sure to rinse well; you don't want to disinfect your horse.

TREATS

If you are like me, you love your horse and the most natural act in the world is to lavish him with a treat just about every time you go out to see him. It gives you a friendly feeling to have him slobbering over your hand as he picks up a tidbit of carrot or apple. The only trouble is that pretty soon he is going to expect those treats to be there, and when he sees your hand near his face he is going to start nibbling. So don't overdo this loving act.

As for sugar, I think you are asking for teeth and digestive problems if you overindulge him in this. If it weren't for lobbies keeping the sugar industry going, the packaging would probably wear a warning label similar to the one on cigarettes.

To treat or not to treat, that is up to you. You would truthfully be better off giving him a loving pat and keeping the food where it belongs—in his feed box at mealtime.

HORSE TALK

Basal feed   Concentrates with less than 16 percent protein.

Bloom   Used to describe a horse's coat in good, healthy condition with a shine, usually due to good feeding habits.

Bran mash   Made by pouring boiling water over bran, usually with some cut-up vegetables, given to a horse that is overly tired or ill.

Bulk   The relationship between the feed's weight and its volume.

Colic   A severe abdominal pain, usually quite serious.

Concentrates   Feeds low in fiber and high in nutrients.

Dry pasture   A pasture that is watered by rain only. Different types of seeds are used than those in an irrigated pasture.

Easy keeper   A term used to describe a horse that stays in good condition without extensive feeding. See THRIFTY.

Feeling his oats   A term used to describe a horse that is unusually "high"—probably due to too much grain and not enough exercise.

Improved pasture   A pasture that is regularly irrigated.

Maintenance   The amount of feed needed to maintain a horse's normal health and function while he is engaged in his own normal activity.

Nutrient   Any food or group of foods having the same general chemical composition, the principal nutrients being protein, carbohydrates, fats, minerals, and vitamins.

Off his feed   Used to describe a horse that is not feeling well and hence not eating normally.

Protein supplements   Concentrates with more than 16 percent protein content.

Ration   The basic amount of food for one twenty-four-hour period.

Roughages   Feeds high in fiber but low in total digestible nutrients.

TDN   Shorthand for "total digestible nutrients," or that part of the feed that is actually utilized in the system.

Thrifty   A term applied to a healthy, active horse that stays in good condition without too much feed. See EASY KEEPER.

3

The Vet Cometh, or Cometh Not

I AM a great believer in preventive medicine, and perhaps even more so in preventing accidents.

A horse is basically a pretty healthy animal. Given the correct immunization program (and it isn't extensive) and an occasional worming, he will come down with far fewer ills than we mortals will. And, as for accidents, one of the national safety organizations has come up with the astounding statement (certainly one I can believe) that 75 percent of all horse-related accidents are caused by carelessness that could have easily been avoided.

PREVENTION IS WORTH . . .

The most frightening word in the horse world is "colic." Colic kills more horses than any other ailment. And it is now believed that up to 90 percent of all colic results from damage done by bloodworms. Moreover, this damage may not be apparent until after the horse has had his bout with colic and become just another statistic.

Worming

All horses have worms of one kind or another. It is the very nature of the beast. The horse eats, drops his manure and then consumes the worms, or their eggs, again as they infest the grass or his bedding; and the more horses you have, the more worms. If you have but one horse you will not need to worm as often, and once a year will probably do it for you— if you have your horse tube-wormed by a vet.

A lot of packaged worm medication is sold over the counter and it would seem that almost all owners do their own worming. One of the reasons often given is that it is too expensive to have a vet come out to worm a horse. This is rather ironic, for in worming their own horses they end up having to do it three or four times a year, and the total cost of the package medication comes to more than the one visit from the vet. Furthermore, when worming is done by the vet you *know* those worms have been taken care of. If you package-worm, you are *never* really sure if your horse has had the correct dosage, or whether or not he has really consumed all of that nasty-tasting stuff. And I don't care what yummy flavors they say it comes in; your horse doesn't read the package; he uses his nose and he knows what's in his feed box. So save yourself and your horse a lot of grief and make an appointment with the vet.

Inoculations

And as long as your vet is there have him give your horse one or more of his yearly boosters.

In the spring your horse will need two injections for eastern and western encephalomyelitis seven to fourteen days apart, and he will need one injection for Venezuelan equine encephalomyelitis (VEE).

In the fall he will need a booster for equine influenza and one for tetanus. If he is new to your stable or you are not sure what inoculation program he has had, you may have to start with the basic program of two injections four to eight weeks apart for both the influenza and the tetanus. Don't skimp. That old bromide "Better safe than sorry" definitely applies here.

Teeth

Do not forget that your vet is also your horse's dentist, and although you may need to see your dentist twice a year, once is enough for friend horse. Your horse is lucky. He doesn't have to worry about cavities, plaque, or malocclusions. What does bother him is the wearing away of his teeth through chewing, so that he sometimes has sharp little ridges that hurt him or prevent him from getting all he should out of his daily ration. If he has this problem the vet may suggest floating his teeth. This merely means that he will file off those sharp edges so that your horse can get back to the business of eating.

Form a Clinic

If you are concerned with money (aren't we all?) and you have some horse-owner friends in your vicinity, you might consider forming a "clinic." What this means is that if you get four or five people together in one spot—say your place—the vet will treat all of your horses and charge for only one house call. Set up one clinic for spring and one for fall and your horse health problems are neatly taken care of.

Injuries

As the safety manuals say, "Most accidents happen at home." This applies to your horse as well. Look around his home for any of the following hazards:

- Sharp protruding objects in his stall, such as nails or pieces of metal that may be coming off the corners or edges of feed boxes, etc.
- Bolts on doors that can be left protruding into openings

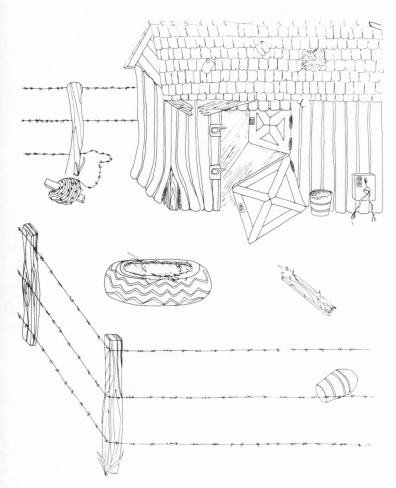

Most accidents happen at home. How safe is your horse's abode?

- Metal buckets and pails with worn, sharp edges or pails used for feeding from which the handles have not been removed
- Sheet-metal siding whose edges have not been nailed in place
- A gate or door that does not close properly and leaves a space through which the horse "thinks" he can fit

- Loose objects, such as cans or rolls of wire, that a horse can put a foot into or through
- Barbed-wire fences
- Any wire fencing in which the horse can paw and catch his leg or foot
- Hidden holes that he might step into
- Old tires used as feeders
- Electrical wires or light fixtures that he can get to with his teeth
- Low beams that he might bump his head on

On the trail use a little caution as well. Do not ride your horse at a rapid gait over territory you cannot see, such as a grassy meadow that could contain a multitude of hidden gopher holes. And when you stop and tie up be sure that it is to something solid.

Be Prepared

Those Boy Scouts know what they are doing. Emergencies do happen, even in the best of households and stables. Thus

A good first-aid kit need not be extensive, but it should be kept up-to-date.

it is wise to equip your tack room with a first-aid kit and a good, concise first-aid book. Keep that kit up to date by examining it often and replacing anything that looks as though it no longer will do the job. And don't rely on learning what to do in case of emergency at the time of the emergency. It might even be a good idea to get a couple of friends together and hold your own first-aid course: practicing putting on various types of bandages and taking your horse's pulse, respiration, and temperature. It is especially important to do the latter when your horse is well so that you will have a basis to go by when you think he is ill.

Your first-aid kit need not be extensive, and a small metal box can easily hold all the supplies you will need. You can obtain the items below from any drugstore or feed store.

- Bottle of mild antiseptic (hydrogen peroxide is good)
- Tincture of iodine
- Ophthalmic ointment
- Antibiotic powder or ointment
- Roll of sterile cotton (10–12 inches wide)
- Roll of surgical gauze (3–4 inches wide)
- Several large square gauze pads (the unsticking kind)
- Roll of adhesive tape
- Two rolls of vet wrap
- Rectal thermometer (with string attached)
- Vaseline

. . . A POUND OF CURE

No one is going to be cheerful all of the time; neither is your horse. However, it may be that he is not feeling too chipper. Any time you suspect this, do not hesitate to take his temperature and check his pulse and respiration just to be sure. Certainly do so if there are the more obvious signs of illness, such as loss of appetite, listlessness, a change in his manure or urine, discharge from his eyes or nose, a cough, or sweating for no apparent reason.

The average temperature of the average horse is 100 degrees. This will vary from 99 up to 101. If it goes over 102 then you may have a problem. To take his temperature, rub some Vaseline on the nub end of the thermometer and insert it carefully into the anus, being sure to stand to one side, should he decide to kick. Try to leave it there for at least three minutes. It is always a good idea to have a string tied to the outside end. They do get lost occasionally.

His rate of breathing should average from twelve to twenty-one respirations per minute. To check this look at the back part of his rib cage and count for one minute. A healthy horse will pause in his breathing every once in a while, as if he were holding his breath. If he is not feeling well he will not do this and his respiration may be as high as forty to fifty per minute.

When checking his pulse look for two things, rate and quality. The normal pulse rate is between thirty-six and forty-eight beats per minute, and it is strong. The easiest way to check his pulse is by feeling the artery on the lower jaw, just in front of the large jaw muscle. But, if you are one of those who have difficulty finding your own pulse, you can put your ear to the near side of his chest just behind his elbow and listen. There is no question that you will find it that way, but with a sick horse I would rather work near his head and know what he is doing all the time.

Take a look at his gums and the white of his eye as well. A healthy horse has good pink gums. If they are yellow and the white of the eye has a yellow tinge, suspect liver trouble.

If your horse is looking in distress at his sides, trying to roll, pawing or sweating, it may be colic, and you had better take a listen as to what is going on inside. Put your ear against his flank—on both sides. If you *do not* hear anything, there is a pretty good chance he has colic. Normal, healthy horses are constantly gurgling as the feed proceeds through their innards.

When in Doubt Call the Vet

Armed with all the facts you can think of, place a call to your vet if you feel there may be something amiss. Be prepared; your vet may also ask you such questions as: "When was the last time he passed any manure or urine and what did it look like? When was the last time your horse ate anything or drank anything? Is there any unusual discharge anywhere?" If you can give your vet an accurate clinical picture of your horse's vital signs, you will be helping both him and your horse. This way the vet can tell pretty much how serious things are and will know what to have you do until he can get there.

If there are two of you, always have someone stay with the horse while you report to the vet. And, if you suspect colic, do not let the horse attempt to roll. The best thing is to keep him moving quietly. If he gets down and rolls he may twist a gut, and that is usually the end of the story.

He's Bleeding!

When a horse bleeds, it looks like a lot—and it can be a lot. But a reassuring thought is that a horse can lose up to three gallons of blood, enough to paint your barn, and still survive.

Wounds are classified into the following categories: *Incised*—those cuts made by metal and other sharp objects, usually deep and serious. *Lacerations*—tears, such as those made by a barbed-wire fence, usually with a flap of skin still attached. *Punctures*—deep closed wounds made with items such as nails or large splinters.

With incised wounds the bleeding can be quite profuse if

either a vein or artery is involved. If this is the case the idea is to stop the bleeding before doing anything else. A pressure bandage is always preferable, but if an artery is involved and the blood is "spurting" you are going to have to apply a tourniquet if it is physically possible. Because these types of wounds usually occur on the legs you should be able to accomplish this. Just be sure to loosen it every half an hour for at least one minute and remove it if the bleeding has stopped.

If bleeding can be controlled by means of a pressure bandage, do so and then do nothing other than wrap the injury and wait for the vet. Nature has designed it so that bleeding cleanses a wound. So if the vet will be coming later you don't have to worry about washing it or putting on any antiseptic. If it will be some time before the vet can get there, you might want to do just a little more and cleanse the wound with a mild antiseptic, though not if it is an arterial wound. *Do not* apply any type of ointment or medication that is not water soluble, or the vet will not be able to clean out the injury. Should the wound be on a leg you can keep the bandage in place by wrapping the area with a layer of cotton and then covering that with vet wrap to hold everything in place.

If the wound is a laceration, with the flap of skin still attached, try to replace the skin where it belongs and bandage it securely. In that way the vet will have a better chance of being able to sew it together when he arrives.

As for puncture wounds, if the object is not causing too much stress and it will not be driven in further, it is sometimes best to leave it in place until the vet comes. It will keep the wound open so that he can insert medication directly as soon as the object is removed and before the wound has time to begin to close.

If, however, the object is in danger of being driven further in, or you are not sure when the vet will come, it would be better to remove it. Puncture wounds are always dangerous, and the important thing is to try to clean it out as much as possible. If the wound is in the foot and your horse will stand

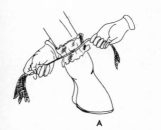

Three basic bandages you should know. A, tourniquet; B, leg; C, foot.

for it, soak his foot in a bucket of water and then pour the entire bottle of antiseptic over the wound. Dry it and pour the iodine into the wound. Make a foot bandage and keep the area as clean as possible.

YOUR VET

If there is one thing this country has a shortage of it is large-animal veterinarians; there is a small-animal clinic on nearly every corner but perhaps only one or two large-animal vets to a county. This is understandable. After all, it is much easier, and not quite so dangerous, to alter a toy poodle in the office than to castrate an untrained colt in the field; and judging from the prices in my area the fee is about the same. Therefore, when you do find your very own vet, take care of him. Do not cry wolf too often and worry him with every little scratch or drippy nose. Use a certain amount of discretion, but not so much that it is too late when you do call him. And remember that he is probably a very overworked individual and very, very busy most of the time. He may be out delivering a breeched calf or inoculating a hundred head of cattle when you call him about Sam's limp. So don't expect him to drop everything and come running every time you call.

If he has a good office staff, and he probably does, they will relay your message to him via car radio as soon as they can and call you back with his instructions. Be prepared to try to cope with your emergency for several hours if need be, and try to stay calm for your horse's sake.

KEEP A RECORD

While you are waiting, write down hour by hour everything that happens—changes in temperature, pulse, and respiration; moods; bowel movements; voiding; anything you think the vet should know.

And speaking of records, you should keep one on every horse you own. These should include inoculations, floating, shoeing, injuries, illness, whatever seems important. A record such as this can be of great help to the vet. It may pinpoint the very reason why your horse is under the weather.

TAKE TWO ASPIRINS

Many times your horse will be beset with little ills and injuries. Learn to cope with these yourself.

A runny eye does not mean he is going blind. It may just be that some chaff blew into it. Apply a little ophthalmic ointment and see if it doesn't clear up in a day, two at the most.

If he has a drippy nose but his temperature and respiration seem normal, he may just have a slight cold. Make sure he is not in a draft and blanket him if it is chilly. Withhold his grain, perhaps giving him a bran mash instead; see that he has lots of fresh water; and let him rest.

If he cuts himself and it is not a gaping wound that is deeper than half an inch, you should be able to handle that yourself. Apply an antibiotic and a square bandage, hold it in place by wrapping it with the gauze bandage, and then vet wrap. If the wound is someplace where you cannot bandage it, apply the ointment or powder and keep it as clean as possible.

As for the aspirins . . . they are for you!

HORSE TALK

Antibiotic   A substance that helps to destroy harmful microorganisms that cause infection.

Antiseptic   A substance capable of destroying the microorganisms that cause septic disease.

Antitoxin   (Example, tetanus antitoxin) A substance that counteracts a toxin or poison.

Bloodworms   The common name for strongyles — a type of worm that sucks blood through the walls of the digestive tract and tends to concentrate in arteries, where their masses slow the blood flow and cause recurring colic.

Ophthalmic   Pertaining to the eye.

Syringe   The barrel part of the hypodermic outfit. Very useful without the needle to irrigate wounds, apply medicine in tight spaces, and get liquid medication down a horse's throat.

Tubing   The method used by veterinarians to get medicine into the horse's stomach. A tube is inserted, through the nose, into the stomach and the medicine pumped directly into the organ.

Twitch   A restraining device used on the horse to keep him still during examination or treatment.

Vet wrap   A long gauze bandage, similar in appearance to an Ace bandage, that is impregnated with a sticky material so that it adheres to itself, thus making a secure bandage.

4

Your Farrier
and You

IT TAKES TWO to do a lot of things and the same goes here. If you want to save money you are going to have to do your part by keeping your horse's feet in good condition so that your farrier will have something other than a disaster area on which to perform his miracles.

GENERAL HOOF CARE

During the winter you worry about thrush; during the summer it's cracking hoofs. So what's an owner to do? Let's examine these two common problems that often beset the horse. For the most part you could say that the villain is moisture, or the lack of it. For a hoof to be in good condition it must be moist, but in the winter it sometimes gets more than its share of moisture, resulting in a nice case of thrush. You then fight it until spring, when the ground, the thrush, and the hoof all dry up . . . and up . . . and up, until suddenly the hoof begins to crack. And you have gone from too much moisture to too little. If you are a purist this may seem to be a bit of an exaggeration, but if you are an exasperated horse owner it is only *God's honest truth!*

Thrush, unless it gets into the advanced stages, is mainly an annoying problem—like athlete's foot. If the cause in your

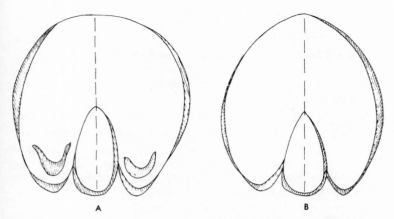

Bottom view of normal front and hind foot. Each requires a differently shaped shoe. A, the front foot is rounded and has a slight fullness on the outside edge; B, the hind foot is narrower and has a pointed toe.

horse is a dirty stall, shame on you. If, however, you are one of those unfortunates (rather your horse is the unfortunate) who must stable your horse in a small paddock that is pure muck much of the winter, you do have a problem. All you can do is treat the thrush, pray for the rains to cease, and plan to relocate before next winter.

There are many commercial medicines on the market, but I am a miser and stick to tincture of iodine or good old household bleach—though it is always best to check with your farrier first just to be sure you are on the right track. He may advise something he feels to be more effective. Those I have suggested are drying agents and somewhat caustic, which helps to remove the dead tissue. They are good for a mild case of thrush. If your horse's case has gone so far that it involves the sensitive tissues I would suggest you either write your will before applying any of the above or call your vet.

Loss of moisture from the hoof is a bad problem but a preventable one. A dry hoof is liable to cracks and breakage. If the horse is standing on hot, dry soil the heat will actually draw the moisture from the hoof. Begin then in the spring to try to maintain the correct moisture balance by applying a hoof dressing once or twice a week—no more. The basic idea of the dressing is to put a layer of protective "grease" on the hoof in order to retard evaporation and keep the drying air out. It should be applied to the entire hoof wall as well as cover the bottom of the foot.

In the summer, depending on what part of the country you live in, you are going to have to add moisture. The best and easiest way to do this is by providing a mud hole in your horse's pasture. Simply dig out a depression next to the water tank and let the water overflow each time you fill it up. He is going to stand there naturally as he drinks, thus absorbing water not only at the top but at the bottom as well.

If he is a stall horse you are going to have to find somewhere to dig a mud hole and tie him there at least an hour each day. And, if you are using shavings as a bedding, you might consider switching to straw or something similar during the hot weather, as shavings will also draw moisture from the hoof.

The ideal hoof is strong, moist, free of cracks and ridges, well shaped, and large enough to support the horse's weight properly. But, like people's fingernails, few are perfect.

LAMENESS

Needless to say you are going to inspect your horse's hoofs often to see that he has not picked up some foreign object that will cause injury and resulting lameness.

As for lameness, I am the type of person to go into immediate panic if I see one of my horses limping even slightly, and my natural reaction is to rush to the phone and call the vet and plead with him to race to my horse's side. This is not to say you should emulate my actions, but do be aware that lameness is not to be taken lightly. Though it may be caused by nothing more than a slight stone bruise, *your vet is the best judge.* Call him and tell him "where it hurts." From your description he can pretty much tell whether or not yours is an

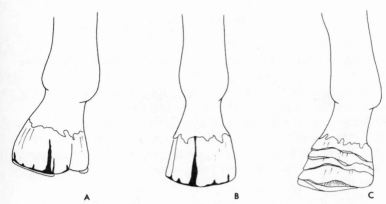

Three bad hoof conditions. A, quarter crack; B, toe or sand crack; C, foundered hoof.

emergency case. Telling where it hurts is not always as easy as it sounds, and to help you locate the area of distress I am including the following hints—pretty reliable most of the time.

- If your horse drops his head when the left front foot hits the ground, it may be the right front leg that bothers him
- If he drops his head when his right front foot hits the ground it may be the left front leg
- If he drops his head when the left hind foot hits the ground, or he drops the right hip, suspect the left hind foot
- If he drops his head when the right hind foot hits the ground, or drops the left hip, look to the right hind leg as the culprit
- If the limping is worse when on soft ground, or he has trouble backing, it is likely the trouble is in his shoulder
- If he has trouble on hard ground, then it may be his feet

Also be sure to note whether the lameness appears to worsen or lessen as he is ridden or warmed up. If it worsens, it may be a bruise or something similar. If it seems to disappear as he is ridden, it could be a strained tendon, ligament, or possibly a torn cartilage.

If the lameness occurs the day after he has been shod, a call to your farrier doesn't hurt. Perhaps he pricked the sensitive tissues of the hoof wall by accident, or there may be a nail that is bearing on a sensitive area, or it may just be that your horse has tender feet because you let him go too long between shoeings. In any case, your farrier will definitely want to know.

FINDING A FARRIER

If you live in the western part of the United States, about everywhere you look you will see trucks and cars decorated with such signs as FREDDIE FARRIER, CORRECTIVE SHOEING A SPECIALTY. A fast guess is that a good percentage of these vehicles are the wandering workshops of "cowboy" horseshoers. Due to poor licensing laws it is possible for a man or woman to take a quickie course in shoeing, or perhaps just read a book, and open his truck for business.

It is not hard to recognize one of these pseudo-farriers once he has shod your horse a couple of times, but it is best to try to avoid this form of discovery. Some of the wrong things that they are noted for include fitting the hoof to the shoe, paring the hoof so that it is neither level nor balanced, cutting the frog, and rasping the wall of the hoof to make it "pretty." (Do not confuse this with rasping the nail ends.)

Actually finding a reliable farrier is not difficult; the hard part is becoming one of his clients.

Check with your horsy friends to see if they have a favorite farrier whom they have been using for some time. Length of professional life in one area is a telltale factor, as cowboy shoers tend not to last more than one season, or else move on to someplace where they are not known. Also check with your vet to see if he will recommend someone. Chances are the same name will enter the conversation. Good farriers get talked about.

Call as soon as possible to set up an appointment. If he is really good you may find yourself waiting several weeks for an opening, and he may even be at the point where he is not taking on any new customers. If that is the case, ask to be put on his waiting list and get his recommendation for someone else. Then track that someone down before *his* client list is filled as well.

THE PROFESSIONAL

A good farrier will take the time to get to know your horse. He will ask you such questions as how often you ride, what type of riding you do, and if your horse has any past history of physical problems. He will then ask you to either ride or show your horse in hand so that he can observe his action and note any problems or deviations that should be taken into consideration.

A skilled farrier can do quite a bit for a horse with conformation faults—and it is because of those faults that the horse usually has problems with his way of going. However,

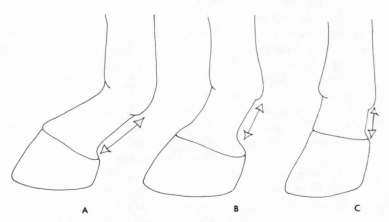

A   B   C

Angle of pasterns. A, sloping; B, normal; C, stumpy.

unless the horse is a youngster under two, any special shoeing will be more of a counteracting aid than a cure. By trimming and weighting he can help to eliminate or reduce paddling, dishing, forging, interfering, speedy cutting, and scalping.

If your horse does have one of these difficulties, the farrier will discuss this with you and perhaps make some suggestions as to "long-term" remediation. (There is no such thing as an overnight correction.)

Only after this analysis will he begin actually to work on your horse.

He will first level all of the feet. Each hoof must be balanced and trimmed level so that when the horse is standing on a hard surface he will be standing squarely on that foot.

The angle of the hoof should be the same as that of the pastern. There are schools that say the foot must be trimmed to a certain degree on the front and another on the hind. Many of these authorities, however, are beginning to agree that the horse is going to travel best the way nature planned for him to travel—with the angle of the hoof the same as the angle of the pastern. And that goes for sloping pasterns as well as stumpy ones, just as long as they are within the realm of the normal.

When the farrier is satisfied that the hoofs are balanced and level he will fit the shoes. They should conform to the bearing surface of the hoof with no air spaces, and the shape of the shoe should correspond to the *natural* shape of the horse's foot—the front feet being naturally rounded while the hind ones are pointed.

Most farriers will make the shoe a little wider at the heels to allow for support as the hoof expands. If the shoe is too narrow at this point, the hoof wall will expand over it in too short a time, thus necessitating reshoeing that much sooner.

The nails should be driven high enough to give a good strong hold and they should all exit at approximately the same distance from the bottom of the hoof; three-fourths of an inch is a good height. Only as many nails should be used as are

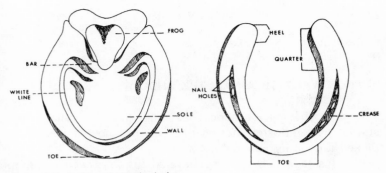

Parts of the sole and standard shoe.

necessary to retain the shoe, usually six, with the toe holes being used only if the shoe cannot be nailed elsewhere owing to a crack or missing chunk of hoof.

So much has been said on the controversy of hot and cold shoeing that one usually comes away confused. Perhaps the best thing to do is to define as simply as possible the two methods and let you make up your mind for yourself.

In cold shoeing a ready-made shoe is modified to fit the foot without the use of heat. This is by far the easiest method of shoeing and enables a lot of people to shoe their own horses with a minimum of tools and training.

In hot shoeing a blank is made to fit the hoof by heating and forming it in a forge. Hot shoes have two distinct advantages. Because they have to be heated in order to bend they can be made of a harder material than the ready-made shoe and will thus last longer. And they are usually applied to the foot for an instant while still smoking hot so that the nail holes are marked on the foot and the farrier knows they are where they should be. *But* therein lies the rub. Some farriers will apply the hot shoe for the purpose of burning the wall in order to make an air-tight fit, rather than taking the time to rasp it flat. With this type of practice considerable damage can be done to the foot by drawing moisture out of the hoof. If you think you see your farrier doing this, question him on it. Perhaps your idea of an instant does not coincide with his idea of an instant.

"FOR WANT OF A NAIL THE SHOE WAS LOST . . ."

A good shoeing job should last until time to reshoe. The staying power of the shoe is one way to know if you have picked a good farrier—but not always!

It is his fault if he has not leveled the hoof well enough; uses nails that don't fit the holes in the shoe; puts the nails in too low, too close together, or so high that they cannot be clenched; or leaves the heels on the front shoes so long that they are pulled off by the hind shoes.

It is your horse's fault if he has a bad pawing habit, gets the shoe caught on a wire fence or on something in his stall.

It is your fault if your horse's hoofs are so dry that the nails break away, or you commit the unpardonable sin of running your horse on pavement or up and down steep hills.

So look for the cause before you decide to look for another farrier.

WHEN TO SHOE

Good farriers keep a record of all their clients and know when they will need new shoes, or trimming, and will set up your appointment schedule accordingly—unless you specify otherwise.

For the first two or three visits, your farrier will probably want to see your horse every six weeks. After observing your horse's growth pattern, wearing pattern, physical problems, any defects, and his general condition, he will suggest a suitable schedule that will keep your horse's feet in riding condition and not be a drain on your coffers. This scheduling will no doubt be heavier in the spring and summer months, with winter being a rest period, if winters are light riding months in your area. He may even suggest pulling the shoes in the fall and continuing with winter care, consisting of a trim every six to eight weeks. This rest period will help to build up and put into good condition any broken or cracked hoofs that have deteriorated because of summer dryness.

You may even be one of the lucky owners who will not need to have your horse shod at all. If you ride your horse only a few hours a week for pleasure and that riding is done on natural turf, you may never need to shoe him. Furthermore, your farrier will be the first one to tell you this! He knows that shoeing is a necessary evil and a barefoot horse will have a healthier hoof. But he will also advise you that you *must* adhere strictly to a good trimming schedule to keep those healthy feet in shape.

THE FARRIER IS COMING

God bless good farriers. Keep them alive and keep them coming! To say the very least, shoeing horses is a mighty dangerous job, and you as an owner should do your best to make your farrier's job a safe one—and in so doing you will keep him coming to your place.

It is your responsibility to train your horse to stand quietly while he is being shod, allow his feet to be handled, refrain from biting and kicking, and learn not to lean on the person handling his feet. All this can be taught as you handle your horse daily while grooming.

Your farrier, if he is a good one, is also a very busy man. When you make that appointment, know that you are going to be home and will have time to get the horse ready and waiting for him. Have the horse caught. With a strong halter and long lead line tie him in an area that is large enough so that the farrier will have plenty of room to maneuver should the horse decide that he does not wish to be shod at that moment. If it is summer, try to find a spot in the shade —a forge and the summer sun are two very hot objects. If it is winter, pick a spot with some protection from the wind and elements.

Make sure your horse's feet are clean and dry, that he has been allowed a drink of water and it is not too near mealtime. And, if it is fly season, put insect repellent on him.

If you have dogs pen them up. Dogs love the cuttings from the hoofs and will dart under a horse or through the legs of the farrier to grab at them. It is only luck that will keep your dog from being stomped on and the farrier from pounding a nail through his thumb. Promise Rin Tin Tin that you will carefully collect all the pieces of yummy hoof and let him have them as soon as the farrier is safely down the drive and heading for his next appointment.

And before he heads down that driveway you might offer him a cool drink or a cup of coffee. It will be much appreciated and you will become one of his preferred customers.

HORSE TALK

Barefoot   Unshod.

Bearing surface   The surface of the shoe that lies against the hoof wall.

Blacksmith   A person who works with iron. A farrier may also be a blacksmith, but a blacksmith is not necessarily a farrier.

Blanks   Unfinished horseshoes that are finished by the farrier in the forge.

Breakover   The point in the horse's stride when the foot leaves the ground and begins its path of flight.

Calk   A projection on the bottom of a horseshoe.

Clinch   That portion of the nail that is bent over where it exits from the hoof wall.

Clip   A portion of the shoe that has been bent upward along the outside to help hold the shoe to the foot.

Cold fitting   Fitting ready-made shoes to the hoof without the use of heat.

Cowboy horseshoer   A shoer with little knowledge of the subject.

Dishing   The turning-in of the foot as it travels forward.

Farrier The professional term for a person who shoes horses.

Fetlock The area directly above and behind the hoof.

Forging Hitting the front shoe with the hind foot as the horse travels forward.

Frog The triangular pad in the sole of the foot.

Horn The insensitive wall of the hoof.

Hot shoeing Fitting the shoe to the hoof by heating the shoe in the forge and bending it to fit.

Interfering Striking one leg with the opposite foot as the horse is moving forward.

Keg shoe A ready-made shoe.

Laminae The leaflike layers within the hoof wall.

Paddling Throwing the front feet outward as the horse moves forward.

Pricking The accidental driving of a nail into the sensitive tissues inside the hoof wall.

Scalping This occurs when the rear pastern comes in under the front foot and hits the toe.

Speedy cutting This is the same as interfering, but the leg is hit above the fetlock.

White line The line visible on the bottom of the hoof which separates the sole from the wall.

5

Tack Can
Be Tacky

WHEN IS a saddle not a saddle? When it fits neither you nor your horse. That goes for any article of tack you ever acquire. Tack is something that should not be obtained in a hurry or on a whim. Every purchase should be carefully considered. Know first of all what you need and why you want that particular piece of tack. Then do a heck of a lot of "window shopping" before you make the final decision to buy.

New or Used?

It makes no difference whether you are a teenager with just enough money to buy a basic bridle and possibly a bare-back pad or have your budget worked out for the full complement of saddle, bridle, accessories, and a New Zealand rug for your steed's winter comfort, you ought to keep the following in mind. Your best buy in any leather or metal item is a *used* one. The reasoning here is that leather and metal are tough substances. Better saddles, bridles, and accessories are made with a quality of leather that is quite durable. Should you be the recipient or purchaser of a new saddle, you will find it sometimes takes *years* to get it broken in to the point where you will have a truly comfortable ride. That is one of the main reasons for getting a used saddle, other than price. Metal also is fairly durable. Visit a museum and take a look at some Roman bits from the first century, should you doubt me.

Cloth and similar substances, on the other hand, will wear out relatively soon and will weaken at points of strain. Furthermore, you will want to have all such items as clean as possible when they're put on your horse. To put a dirty saddle pad, which someone else's horse has been using, on your horse is like your putting on someone else's dirty socks. *New* is the word here.

A SADDLE IS FOREVER

A good saddle can last you a lifetime. I have a seventy-eight-year-old friend who is still a practicing horse trainer. He is using the same saddle day in and day out that he purchased in 1932. If you should ask him, he could not begin to tell you how many horses have been under that saddle, and if you should ask him further if he is considering buying a new one, he will tell you, "Heck, no! I've just got this one broke in." That, dear readers, is a voice of experience. Pay attention to it!

What to Look For

Most good riding shops carry a line of used saddles. There and the bulletin board of your favorite riding academy are the first places to begin your "window shopping." A shop that you can trust is a good place to start as it will not take on any saddle to sell that has a broken tree or damaged fittings. Your purchase price, however, will include the commission the store charges the seller for the sale.

If you should consider buying a saddle from a private individual, first check to see that the tree is in good shape. With the saddle lying on its side, press your hand against the side of the saddle just above the knee roll. Then, with the saddle on a rack, put one hand on the cantle and one on the pommel and press firmly downward. You should not feel any unnatural give at either point. Also check the billets, or straps, that are used to attach the saddle to the girth. They should be pliable, well attached, and not too worn at any point. Check the stitching on the saddle proper, both on the top and the underneath sides. It is true that stitching can be repaired by a good craftsman, but if it is worn at a point where you can see it, it may be worn at some hidden point, and that is where it is bound to give at the wrong time—usually when you are at the top of a jump.

On threat of losing international good will, I would strongly advise against buying an Argentine saddle. You may be tempted, as they look, to the untrained eye, almost as good as the more expensive saddles and are about one-fourth the price. But you need only to ride one for a few moments to understand the tremendous difference between the cheaper saddle and the one in which a lot of know-how has gone into the making. The quality saddle will almost mold you into the correct balance and contact with your horse.

Fit

When you do find a saddle that is to your liking, ask if you can take it home so that you may try it on your horse. If what you are buying is a used saddle you will probably have no trouble in this respect, but if the saddle is new, the owner might be somewhat hesitant, fearing a scratch or similar catastrophe.

A saddle that doesn't fit your horse properly will cause him nothing but trouble, which in turn will mean trouble for you. When trying out a saddle always use a clean white towel between the saddle and your horse. This not only keeps the saddle from becoming soiled but it will help you to locate any point that is causing too much pressure, such as across the withers or spine. When mounted, stand and put your full weight in the stirrups. There should be room enough to insert two fingers between the pommel and the withers. If there is more, the possibility is that the saddle may be too narrow for the build of your horse and will consequently slip around rather than settle properly into place. This will not only be uncomfortable for your horse but dangerous for you. If there is too little room under the pommel, it is likely that the saddle is pressing elsewhere as well and will cause sores or tender spots on his back. Ride enough to work up a light sweat under the saddle and then check any marks on the towel.

Some saddles are designed especially for certain breeds, such as the narrow-backed Arab or the broad-backed Morgan. If you have one of these breeds definitely look for that type of saddle. Otherwise make sure that you are *not* buying one made for a kind of horse that you don't own.

Now for *your* fit. A sixteen-inch saddle is suitable for a child or very small-boned woman, while a nineteen-inch one is designed to fit a large man. If you are of average build you should try to get one in the seventeen- to eighteen-inch size range. Sizes vary from make to make and style to style, so you should not forgo looking at one saddle just because it may be a different size from the one that fit you somewhere else. The size measurement is taken from the nailhead on either side of the pommel to the center of the cantle.

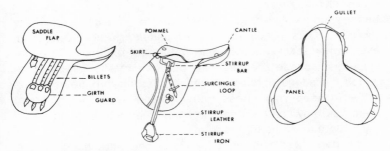

Parts of the English saddle.

TYPES OF SADDLES

By now you are probably pretty well set as to which style of riding is for you—flat saddle or stock saddle—so there will be no discussion as to the merits of one type over the other. We'll discuss instead how to get the best for your money in the type you have settled on.

The English or Flat Saddle

There are three major types of English saddle: the forward-seat, the park saddle, and the all-purpose model.

The Germans, Italians, and French are the foremost makers of the forward-seat saddle. A good Stubben, Pariani, or Hermes saddle on your horse will mark you as a knowledgeable horseman. When looking for a park saddle you might do well to seek out a Crosby, made in England. Crosby also makes a good all-purpose one, as does Passier of Germany.

The *forward-seat saddle* is used mainly for riding hunters and jumpers and in hunt-seat equitation. It is probably the most popular style of flat saddle ridden today. The deepest part of the seat is in the center, placing the rider in the forward position. Padded knee rolls keep the rider's knees in place when traveling over rough country or over jumps. The better saddles also have a padded roll behind the area where the calf comes in contact with the saddle, giving the rider an even firmer seat. Saddles come with knee rolls made of either smooth or suede leather. The purpose of the suede is to match the suede patches on the insides of your breeches, in order to keep your knees from slipping. I personally prefer them, but they can be a pain to keep clean and in good shape if you do a lot of riding in the rain.

The *park saddle* is used for riding the park horse of any breed, the Saddlebred and the Walking horse. It is designed to show off the horse's high action in front by keeping the rider's balance behind the action. Some are cut back three to four inches at the pommel to give the horse a longer look and allow for a higher neck carriage. Riding this form of saddle takes a lot of learning. It does not allow for a secure seat and is definitely a saddle designed for ring use rather than trail.

The *all-purpose* saddle is a little heavier and has a deeper seat than the forward-seat saddle, though it is quite similar and is ridden with a balanced seat. It is used for dressage, cross-country, and endurance riding.

FITTINGS

The fittings of English saddles are interchangeable, so if they are not to your liking you can buy others. The girth is

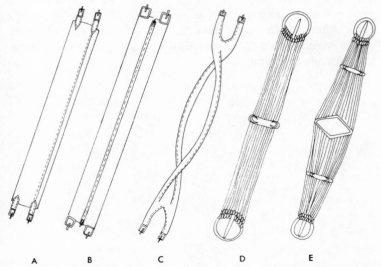

A   B   C   D   E

Girths. A, *English folded leather;* B, *English Fitzwilliam;* C, *English Balding;* D, *Western string;* E, *Western roping (good for regular use as it distributes the strain on your horse).*

made of leather. If you care about your horse and live in a hot climate, you will get one made of mohair for summer riding—though you *never* use it in the show ring. There are several types of girths but the better ones are shaped at the elbows to prevent chafing and are padded for your horse's comfort. Those with elastic inserts at either one or both buckle ends will allow your horse more freedom to breathe.

New stirrup leathers can be bought if those on the saddle are not long enough. The fit of the stirrups themselves is extremely important. They should not be so large that your foot can slip through and be hung up if you have a fall, nor should they be so small that your foot can become wedged and cause a similar accident. A good size is one inch larger than the sole of your boot. Stirrup pads are a nice addition. They keep your foot from slipping about in wet weather and keep the cold metal from coming in contact with your boot during freezing weather.

While we are discussing stirrups I would like to mention a point of safety that is often ignored. If you are not yet an experienced horseman, it is a good idea to leave the safety bar of your stirrup catch *open* so that the leather can slip off easily should you have a fall. Better to lose a stirrup leather occasionally than your life.

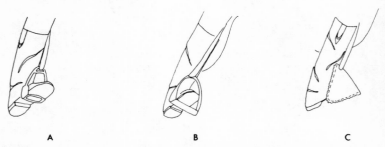

A   B   C

English stirrup irons. A, regular; B, offset; C, foot cover for cold weather.

The Western or Stock Saddle

The basic difference between today's stock saddle and the one used by cowboys of old is that today's saddle is built for the balanced seat. If you watch an old-timer ride he will usually be a bit behind the action of the horse. There was a reason for this. He spent many hours in the saddle, and this was, for him, the most comfortable way to ride. That is the reason why the cantles of those old saddles were so high —to keep him in place if his horse made a sudden move. But today there is basically no difference between the seat of the stock-saddle rider and that of the forward-seat rider.

The tree of the stock saddle is made in three basic types: the full Quarter Horse tree, which fits most Quarter Horses and heavier stock-type horses with full shoulders and low withers; the semi–Quarter Horse tree for horses with some-what higher withers; and the Arabian tree for the smaller, narrower-backed horse.

The swells, or fork, also come in three types: the narrow one used for roping, the extremely wide angular one for cutting, and the general-purpose one. The general-purpose swell is the type you will be looking for and is the kind seen on show saddles.

It is best not to buy a saddle with a seat, padded or un-padded, that is built up in front. These are designed for com-fort but do not allow the rider to shift his weight forward and maintain the correctly balanced seat, a necessity in any equitation or performance class.

The way the stirrups are hung is also important. They should be farther forward than the deepest part of the seat and hung so that they will move freely with the movement of your legs.

A mohair cinch is the only kind of front cinch to use with a stock saddle. Preferably it should be wide and always in good condition—neither dirty nor worn to the point of being dangerous. The girth should be long enough so that when the horse is saddled the rings of the girth come equally up about halfway between the saddle and the horse's elbows.

Should you have a saddle with both front and rear cinch be sure to have a cinch spacer—that is, a little strap that goes between the front and rear cinch underneath the horse's belly. Without it your rear cinch will slip back, and you may soon be the owner of one of the finest bucking horses in your territory.

Determine the soundness of the tree when buying a used saddle. Also check to see that all latigo and other leathers used for attaching and tying are sound and pliable, not hard and brittle and ready to break. And the sheepskin lining, if worn, should be worn smoothly and evenly all over.

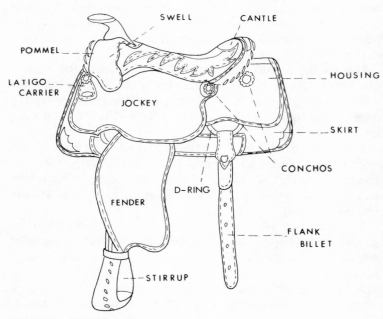

Parts of the Western saddle.

The measurement of the stock saddle is made from the center of the fork to the cantle, the usual size being fifteen inches. Naturally they come in longer seats for larger people and smaller seats for youngsters.

For a Western saddle stick to the American-made saddle. Some of the finest stock saddles in the world are made in New Mexico and Arizona.

As a native Westerner I feel I must warn you against one mistake that many people make when visiting the Southwest. Just over the border in Mexico one of the main tourist attractions is the leather shop. Here you will find what appear to be some of the most beautifully carved saddles you have ever seen. True, the carving is beautiful, but it is usually done on inferior-grade leather and sometimes built on a tree that is green. A green tree will eventually dry, as all wood does, producing some rather astounding results and a ruined saddle.

If the riding you are planning on doing is mostly cross country or through brush you would be better off buying a roughout saddle. The roughout leather does not show the scratches that carved or plain leather does and actually gets better looking the more it is used; similar to the patina on a good piece of silver. On the other hand, if you are planning on doing any showing at all, you will want to buy a more elaborate, carved saddle; and if you really get into showing you will probably end up buying a saddle to use strictly for show purposes in addition to your everyday one.

Show saddles are beautifully made, with varying amounts of silver adorning them. A good used show saddle is usually a bargain, as most people take excellent care of them, and they are the first piece of tack to go when the seller is in need of a little money. Silver can be added to your show saddle at any time, with such ornamentation as silver horn caps, corner pieces, and name plates. Just don't overdo it or you will look as if you belonged in a parade class rather than an equitation or pleasure class.

Although not strictly a part of the saddle, there are a couple of appointments that belong on every show saddle and *are* required in the show ring. One is a *reata*. This is a small, braided leather rope to be attached to the part of the saddle where a working rope would go. And if you ride in California and other nearby areas you will be using what is known as a *romal* rein, a combination closed rein and quirt made of braided leather. Because this is a closed rein, and to make up for not having split reins to ground-tie your horse, you must carry hobbles. These are either tied to the back of the saddle with the saddle strings or fastened through the near side opening on the skirt, where the rear cinch would go. Furthermore, if the strings on the rear of the saddle are not used to tie the hobbles they must be formed into tight little coils (similar to those new clothesline rope comes in from the store), not left to dangle loosely. If you are buying a used saddle, all of these will come already properly arranged, and you need only take it home and put it on your horse.

As you can see these saddles can become very expensive items, and a good place for them is on a handsome wooden saddle rack in your family room or den rather than in a tack room, where they can gather more than their fair share of dust and grime and the attention of thieves. Too, they are not a bad conversation piece for your nonhorsy friends.

BAREBACK PADS

This innovation is both a blessing and a curse—a blessing in that it sure beats sitting on that old backbone and a curse in that so many unfortunate accidents have occurred because of it.

A hefty percentage of young riders will spend much of their time on this rig. If you are one, please pay attention to a couple of very important points before you go out and spend your allowance on that pretty plaid but ill-fitting pad, instead of the more safe but icky-green one.

First of all, if you are looking at the type where the girth is sewn onto the pad, it *must fit* your horse. There is no safe way to make one smaller that is too big. You would be surprised how many are taken home only to have the buyers find out that they were meant for something the size of a Percheron.

Second, make sure that the webbing of the girth is of good material and not weak at any point (the minute it begins to show anything more than normal wear you should get rid of it).

Third, should you decide to buy a bareback pad with stirrup attachments, make sure that there is some sort of safety release, not merely round rings that will hold you to the horse if you have to tumble and your foot is hung up in the stirrup. If you can't find one with this safety factor, you are better off forgoing the stirrups and learning a little better balance, so that you can stay put without them.

And, when you do buy that pad, remember that it sits next to your horse's hide and must be washed as often as you would wash any saddle pad. Most of them will go nicely through a washer; just don't forget to take off the stirrup leathers first.

BITS, BRIDLES, AND HACKAMORES

The science and knowledge of the bit is so extensive that it is difficult to know where to begin when attempting to discuss it. One should not really generalize, but that is what I am about to do.

A bit and bridle along with various accouterments are used to control the horse. The wrong bit in the wrong hands can literally destroy a horse's mouth and/or temperament. In the right hands almost any bit can be used to control a horse beautifully—but that means the *right* hands. If you are a beginner or semi-experienced horseman you are better off, both for your horse's sake and your own, to use the bit that your horse has been accustomed to, if he goes well with it

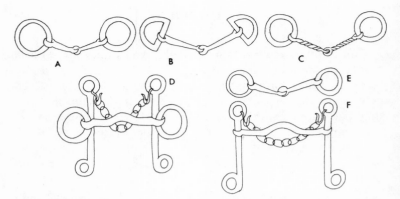

English bits. A, regular snaffle; B, egg butt snaffle; C, twisted wire snaffle; D, Pelham; E, bridoon; F, curb. The bridoon and curb, also known as a "bit and bridoon," are used together in the full bridle.

and it is not so severe that there is danger of ruining his mouth should you accidentally jerk on it or use a heavy hand. If your horse is not going well in what has been used on him, a discussion with a trainer or experienced rider, rather than random experiments, will save you money in the long run and a lot of grief for your horse.

English Bits and Bridles

There are basically three types of bits and bridles used by the English rider: the snaffle, the full double bridle, and the pelham.

THE SNAFFLE

The snaffle is the mildest of all bits. It consists of a bar jointed in the middle, with rings of varying sizes at each end to which the cheek pieces are attached. The main control action is on the corners of the mouth and bars. The larger the mouthpiece and the larger the rings the milder the bit. The severest snaffle is one with a twisted wire mouthpiece.

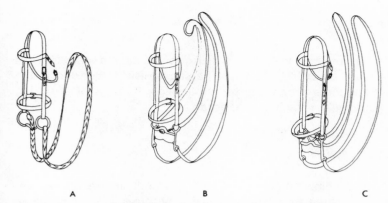

English bridles. A, hunting snaffle; B, Pelham; C, full or double bridle.

The snaffle can be a very effective bit and makes an excellent training device. In some regions it is called a "colt bit," being the first one the horse is introduced to. Some horses have such good mouths and temperament that they will spend their entire days in the snaffle. Hunters are often shown in this bit, and working hunters are ridden much of the time in them.

A wide rein is used, which is usually laced or plaited to help the rider keep a firm grip in inclement weather. This is called a hunting rein.

THE DOUBLE BRIDLE

When the snaffle, called a *bridoon* in this case, is used in conjunction with a curb bit it is called a *full double bridle,* or *bit and bridoon.*

The curb bit acts on the bars of the horse's mouth. It has a solid mouthpiece and straight shanks, or side pieces. A curb chain is used in conjunction with the bit and acts as a fulcrum to put pressure on the mouth. A lip strap keeps the horse from pulling the shank of the bit into his mouth or tossing it up over his nose. The snaffle rein is usually an eighth of an inch wider than the curb rein. Widths depend upon your personal preference, but the narrower reins are easier for a woman or child to handle. The snaffle rein is buckled in the center. This allows it to be run through the rings of a running martingale, should one be used.

THE PELHAM BRIDLE

This combination of a snaffle and curb in one bit has become extremely popular, probably because it is far easier to handle than the full bridle. The top ring of the bit serves as the snaffle while the bottom ring utilizes the action of the curb. The same kind of reins are employed here as are used on the full bridle.

In the better-quality bridles the reins and cheek pieces are sewn to the bits. If you have a choice between buying a new inferior-grade bridle, such as a school bridle, and a used one that originally cost four times as much, by all means get the older but better one, as long as it is in good condition. Undo the buckles and look for signs of wear and bend the leather to make sure it is supple. Quality bridles like quality saddles will hold up for many years if well taken care of.

Western Bits and Bridles

The Western rider uses basically the curb. Though this is a harsher bit, it is well advised, as the Western horse is ridden on a much looser rein than his English counterpart. The Western curb differs from the English one in that the shanks are curved backward from the mouthpiece toward the horse. A curb strap is more often used instead of a curb chain, or one with a combination chain and strap.

In some bits the shanks are not fixed to the mouthpiece. This allows the bit to be more flexible and lessens the severity of side rein movement.

Many people use a bit that has what is called a *cricket* or *roller* attached within the port. This acts as a pacifier and helps produce more saliva in the horse's mouth. The more saliva the horse produces the easier it is for him to tolerate the bit. Some rollers are made of copper to further increase the flow. These bits are known as cricket or roller bits. The pacifier idea certainly seems to work. Listen to any horse outfitted with one; he will play with it by the hour. Roller bits are not to be confused with spade bits.

The idea of the spade bit is complex and most people feel it is cruel. On a horse that has not been properly conditioned and trained it would be, because of its design. The philosophy of the bit's use has come to us through the old Spanish school, and it is used extensively by fine trainers on the West Coast. Its use is in conjunction with hackamore training. In the hands of a horseman experienced in this type of riding it can achieve a unification of horse and rider other-

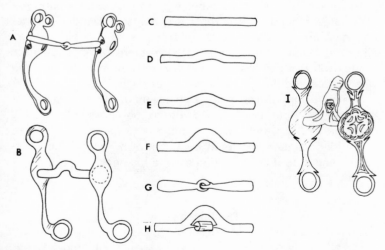

Western bits. A, *loose jaw snaffle;* B, *curb;* C, *plain port;* D, *low port;* E, *medium port;* F, *high port;* G, *snaffle;* H, *cricket;* I, *spade bit.*

wise not readily attainable; but *only* in the hands of such a rider and *only* on a properly trained horse.

The split-eared bridle has become very popular in the West and is used as both a working bridle and a show bridle. As a working bridle it consists of a plain or braided leather headstall with holes for the right ear or both ears. It occasionally comes equipped with a throatlatch as well, although that seems to take away from the simplicity of the bridle, which is its main feature.

The show bridle is made of round or flat leather and adorned with silver. This bridle is quite handsome, as it does not detract from the natural beauty of the horse's head.

The other form of bridle is similar to the English snaffle bridle and includes a noseband, browband, and always a throatlatch.

The type of reins used differs not so much with the type of bridle as with the area in which you live. In California and parts of the Southwest they will almost always be of the *romal* type mentioned earlier, and to appear in a Western class in this area with any other type of rein would mark you as strange indeed. These reins are made of braided leather and can be quite elaborate, with knots and silver added. They are usually expensive, but if they are taken good care of they will last you many, many years. They must be cleaned with a good saddle soap and are never oiled.

The split rein is used more extensively in all other areas of the country. Split reins are made to be loose and should never be tied together. Their purpose is to ground-tie a horse if the rider should dismount or be thrown—which they certainly cannot do if they are tied around his neck.

The Hackamore

There are two types of hackamores, the *bosal* and the *mechanical hackamore,* which is sometimes referred to as a

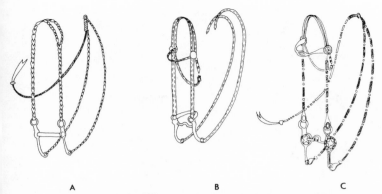

Western bridles. A, braided split-ear with roping rein and romal; B, full with split reins; C, silver-mounted show with closed rein and romal.

hackamore bit. Both could be put into the class of training devices, but some horses are ridden all of their lives in one.

The *bosal* has come to us from the Spanish school of training, where it was used first to train the young horse in the basic rudiments of reining. It works on the outside part of the jawbones, which have a thin covering of skin and are thus quite sensitive. The horse was then finished off with the spade bit.

The hackamore bit is quite often used by gymkhana riders and barrel racers who need to make fast turns and stops and do not want to destroy their horses' mouths. It has also grown in favor among the younger set, who sometimes are saddled with a horse whose mouth has been hardened beyond any use of a regular bit.

The mechanical hackamore puts a squeezing action on the nose and pressure on the curb grove. Caution should be taken on two points. One, that the noseband does not drop too low on the horse's nose, so that his breathing is cut off. (Horses cannot breathe through the mouth, and no air—no horse!) Second, that your curb strap or chain is not too tight, so that it causes undue pressure and pain.

And before you buy a horse unable to go in any other head gear, keep in mind that hackamores are prohibited in almost all horse-show classes.

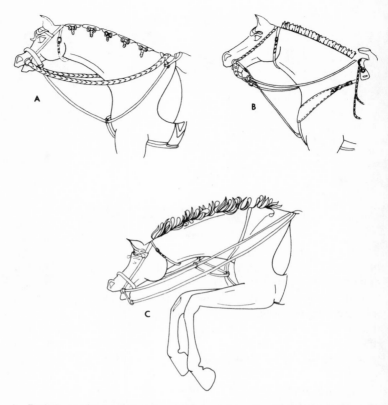

A, *English standing martingale and breastplate;* B, *Western tie-down and breast collar;* C, *English running martingale.*

MARTINGALES AND TIEDOWNS

These are artificial aids used in keeping down the head of the horse that tends to stargaze. They should be considered as training devices, to be used only until your horse can learn to keep his head where it should be.

The English rider uses the martingale, of which there are two types. The standing martingale is attached to the back of the cavesson, while the running martingale is forked and has rings through which the snaffle reins are run. Because the running martingale bears on the mouth, only an experienced rider should use it.

The tiedown is the Western equivalent of the standing martingale. In the West it is also used by barrel racers and gymkhana riders.

None of these devices is allowed in pleasure-horse or equitation classes. By all means, if your horse does not actually require one, don't buy one.

BREASTPLATES

Whether you ride English and call it a breastplate or ride Western and call it a breast strap or collar, this piece of equipment serves one purpose—to keep the saddle from slipping backward. It is useful if you have a horse so built that this tends to happen when going over a jump or up a hill. If your horse or your style of riding makes this piece of tack an unnecessary purchase, for heaven's sake do not spend your money on it. The simpler you keep your horse's wardrobe the better for everyone, especially that overburdened piece of equipment—your wallet.

HALTERS AND LEAD ROPES

I refuse to enter the controversy as to whether or not you should leave a halter on a horse when he is in his stall or paddock. Fight that out among yourselves. But I am going to stress the point that you need not one but *two* halters—one to lose and one to find. Ditto lead ropes.

A leather halter for everyday use has pretty much gone out of style. Not only is it difficult to keep clean but it becomes stiff with use, if only because the horse is going to be wearing it in all types of weather. Moreover, there is such an array of less-expensive and more-serviceable halters now available that I see no reason for buying any other kind. If you choose one of the rainbow-hued nylon-webbed ones, make sure it has a snap on the cheekpiece so that you won't always have to be doing and undoing the buckle, which can sometimes be quite stiff. I personally prefer a rope halter, which can be easily removed in case of emergencies and is relatively cheap. The Johnson halter is a favorite of mine. It is known for its strength and durability. There are cheaper versions on the market, but each time I have bought one I have been sorry, as they have broken at the most inopportune times.

Your lead ropes should be *strong* and *long* enough to really work with.

If you plan to do any showing at halter, do wait until you can afford a proper show halter and lead—else beg or borrow one. If you appear in any but a weekly get-together in a work halter you are going to feel pretty silly.

Show halters, like show bridles, can be very elaborate, but I think it is a mark of good taste to buy one of the simpler ones. The idea is to show your horse's head off to his best advantage, and if it is covered with silver gunk you are going to defeat that purpose.

SADDLE BLANKETS AND PADS

The old standard saddle pad for the English rider used to be made of felt or sheepskin. Modern science has now come up with something far superior to both, and the price is right. I cannot see buying a pad made of anything other than Equi-fleece, either single- or double-faced. This material is light-weight, absorbs perspiration, and can be thrown in the washer and dryer and be back on your horse within an hour. The pads come in white and yellow, but I think the white looks better on almost any color horse. They are suitable for both everyday riding and show. Be sure that the one you buy fits the contour of your saddle with about an inch showing all around. The park saddle rider does not use a pad, at least in the ring.

Equi-fleece has even entered the Western world, but it has one disadvantage in that it is rather light for the heavier Western saddle. For everyday wear you might consider using it in combination with a heavy hair pad. A double Navajo wool or cotton blanket is also an excellent choice.

For show purposes there is a variety of blanket with a corona or decorative roll, but for some reason this always reminds me of Roy Rogers. A nice Navajo blanket is just as eye-catching and shows a more workmanlike attitude on the part of the rider.

YOUR HORSE'S BOOTS

The average horseman need concern himself with only two types: the bell boot and the skid boot.

The purpose of the bell boot is to protect the coronet area of the front feet from being cut by the rear hoofs when the horse is landing from a jump. They are relatively inexpensive and a good idea should you be doing any amount of jumping.

If you have a stock horse and plan on practicing sliding stops, you might invest in skid boots. These are worn on the hind ankles to protect the fetlocks from injury when executing a sliding stop.

SADDLE BAGS AND CASES

Although a nice set of leather saddle bags is one of the most useful accessories you can own, it is not necessary to have these before you can plan on a picnic or other outing. For the Western rider there is now available from most catalog houses a plastic saddle pouch. This is a zippered bag made to fit just behind the cantle of your saddle and tied on with the saddle strings. It is lined with waterproof plastic and is large enough for a good-sized lunch plus camera or what-have-you.

For the English rider there are sandwich cases that buckle onto the two little D's on the near side of the saddle—that's right, that's what those are there for.

SHEETS AND BLANKETS

If you are the owner of a horse that is capable of growing his "own blanket," that is the best kind. Don't clip him! Let him grow it out and Nature will protect him far better than you ever will. After all, will she forget to put on his blanket on the very night that the biggest blizzard since '88 hits?

If, however, you have fallen heir to a horse with thin skin and a fine coat and live in the colder regions of the country, you will have to break down and purchase a blanket for him.

Buy only the best you can afford. Cheap bargains will never last past the first couple of rolls. They are going to split every time. Get one made with a good, heavy hose-duck cover and lined with wool or kersey. They come in sizes just like your clothing and you must know the height of your horse when setting out to buy one. Also make note of the

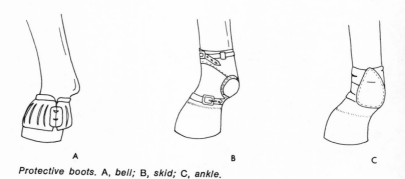

Protective boots. A, bell; B, skid; C, ankle.

shape of your horse's withers, and if they are prominent, get one with a cut-back neck. The ones with the straps that cross underneath the belly somehow seem to stay on a bit better than the others. But, if you continue to have trouble, get a surcingle. This is like a belt and will keep that blanket in place. Have your blanket professionally cleaned at a horse laundry each spring and store it away with mothballs.

As for sheets, you will need one if you plan to do any showing in the spring, even if your horse was not blanketed during the winter months. Let him wear it at night as he begins to shed out. It will start the hair lying a bit smoother and keep him warm should there be a sudden cold snap. This is also quite important if you clip him rather than wait for the shedding process to complete itself. A sheet is also essential for putting on him the day of the show. After you have gone to all the trouble of making him handsome, you don't want him to get dirty, do you?

One word of caution: if your horse is a pasture horse and it rains on him, get that wet blanket or sheet off as soon as you can and get it dried out. Keep him warm and out of drafts while you are doing it—even if it means putting the family car outside and the horse inside the garage.

Unless you are the owner of a race horse or blue-blooded Saddlebred, don't worry your head about buying hoods, coolers, and the like. Pampered horses, like pampered children, are hard to keep in line.

CARE OF TACK

I may be running in the wrong social circles, but I don't have one single acquaintance who has access to a groom, and I am willing to bet you don't either. That means the dirty work falls to you. Nor am I so naïve that I think you are going to take your tack completely apart each time it is used and clean it. Let us then settle on the least amount of activity that your conscience will tolerate and still keep your tack from aging too quickly.

Putting up your tack properly each time you ride is half the battle. Keep a sponge in the tack room and wipe off any area of the saddle or bridle that has come in contact with the horse or is muddy. Hang the bridle up by the crown so that all leathers fall straight, and clean the bit.

If yours is an English saddle, run the stirrups up and completely undo the girth and lay it across the top of the saddle. If it is a Western saddle and still a bit new, run a broom handle or stick through the stirrups so that they are held in an outward position. Cover your saddle with a towel or cloth feed sack to keep the dust from settling into the leather. Shake or brush out your saddle pad, and place it so that it will air out completely before you use it again.

If you ride three or four times a week a good cleaning once a month should suffice—at least it is better than none at all. Pick a night when there's nothing good on TV or when you are looking for an excuse not to do the budget.

Start with the bridle. Take it completely apart. If it is a complicated one and you haven't done it before, I suggest you number the parts (use bits of masking tape) so you know where all those straps go when they are lying in a mass of confusion on the kitchen table. Using a squeezed-out sponge and your saddle soap, clean each piece thoroughly. If you work up a lather your sponge is too wet. Dry each piece with a soft towel and then, using another rag, apply a thin film of neatsfoot oil. Clean all the metal parts and polish them with a good metal polish. Now reassemble the whole thing before anything gets lost, courtesy of the family cat or dog. Remember that you never oil braided leather items, such as *romal* reins.

Follow the same procedure with your saddle, but do not put oil where you will sit. On an English saddle, you should remove the stirrup leathers, inspect them for wear, and reverse them—that is, put the near one on the off side and vice versa. This is like switching your sheets so that the wear is evenly distributed.

If it is a Western saddle you are not going to be removing anything, but do take the time to look for any wear that you might otherwise miss.

Use wooden matches or toothpicks to clean out stirrup holes and deep carving.

Help for the New Tack Owner

At this point, *do you need help!* The best thing I can think of is to throw anything new in a vat of neatsfoot oil for about twenty-four hours and hope for the best. Truly, this is the best way to handle new leather items except for saddles. Soak them and then dry them and use gloves for riding for the next few weeks. The oil will turn any light-colored leather dark— that is what you want anyway. Riding with new tack is like wearing a new pair of Levi's—no one does it.

For an English saddle, just ride it a lot and use neatsfoot oil on the areas that do not come in contact with your clothing.

As for the Western saddle, I wouldn't trade places with you for a ton of hay. Unless you are knock-kneed and pigeon-toed those stirrups are going to hang at a forty-five-degree angle from where you want them until they are broken in—one to three years from now depending on how often you ride. Once a day you must sponge the insides of the fenders with water and then set them to the degree you want them by running a broom handle through them as the saddle rests on the saddle rack. There is no easy way out. My best to you and *good luck!*

HORSE TALK

Appointments   Equipment and clothing used in a specific event, class, or style of riding.

Billet straps   The straps on an English saddle with which the girth is attached.

Cavesson The noseband, with attaching headpiece, of an English bridle.

Cinch The band that holds the saddle to the horse. More often used to describe Western tack. (See GIRTH.)

Concho A decorative silver piece on a Western saddle or bridle. Often used to cover the area where leathers are joined.

Crownpiece The part of the bridle that goes over the top of the horse's head.

D's Rings attached to the saddle and used for attaching other tack onto, such as latigo straps, breastplates, etc.

Girth The band that holds the saddle to the horse. More often a word used to describe English tack. (See CINCH.)

Headstall The leather pieces of the bridle with the exception of the bit and reins.

Hobbles A strap or rope formed so that it holds the front legs of a horse to keep him from straying too far from camp. Show hobbles are elaborately braided affairs.

Latigo strap A long leather strap used to attach the cinch to the Western saddle.

Longe line A long line used to exercise or train a horse with the person standing still and the horse circling around him.

Noseband The strap that goes over the nose on a Western bridle. (See CAVESSON.)

Outfit The tack or equipment of a Western horseman.

Romal The quirt part of a type of reins used in the West. The entire reins are commonly called *romal reins* although properly they should be referred to as *closed reins* with a *romal* attached.

Shank That part of the bit from the mouthpiece down. Also a lead line in which there is a length of chain at the halter end.

Surcingle A broad band, beltlike, that is used to keep a blanket or sheet in place.

Tack The equipment used in riding and handling a horse.

Tapadera A stirrup cover; used in the West to protect the feet from brush. On parade saddles they are a prominent part of the saddle and highly decorated.

Tree The wooden (hence tree) frame on which the saddle is built. Now sometimes made of fiberglass or plastic.

War bridle An emergency bridle in which a rope is tied around the horse's lower jaw. Should not be used unless absolutely necessary.

6

Trailers and Trailering

I AM GOING to make a confession. I hate trailering! I probably hate it as much as any horse. And I have a feeling that I have a lot of kindred spirits in this respect. Whenever I get behind a steering wheel and see in the rear mirror that thing that is about to follow me down the road I cringe. Nor can I understand any horse with any respectable amount of intelligence voluntarily entering into that metal box and allowing himself to be driven onto the suicidal territory of the American highway system.

Perhaps it is because I have been witness to some rather grisly accidents involving trailering that this feeling persists even after twenty-odd years of dragging a trailer to shows and meets. Or perhaps it is because I have a yellow streak hidden under my hunt coat. Whatever the reason, when I decided to write this chapter my first thought was *safety . . . safety . . . safety!*

WHAT TO LOOK FOR IN A TRAILER

Buying a trailer is a large investment in anyone's budget and sometimes a used one may be a good buy.

Although there are several types of trailers, the type a goodly percentage of the populace uses is a two-horse, tandem trailer. Two-horse because you will probably end up with more than one horse eventually, or you will be taking someone else with you to the show. After all, the idea now is to share the ride and save gas. Tandem because that means it has two axles and four wheels, which makes it a lot easier to pull and a lot safer.

Despite what the advertising media tell you, new products are *not* always the best products. A seven- or eight-year-old trailer in good condition could be a better buy even at near the price of a new one. Horse trailers hold their value and are in great demand. Thus you are not going to find a used one hanging around every corner waiting to be bought. But it is certainly worth the effort to try to locate one before you sign the contract on a new one.

USED-TRAILER CHECK LIST

When you do locate your horse's future transportation system, there are a few points that should be checked to make sure it is a safe means of travel for him.

Floorboards   These are of great importance and must be solid and free of any rot. Pull up the floor mat and check. Also look at the underside of the trailer.

If you doubt the importance, imagine yourself driving along the highway at fifty or sixty miles an hour and suddenly the floor gives way—your horse with it—and you continue to drive on, possibly for miles, unaware of what has happened. Not a pretty picture? You're right! But one seen often enough to make it one of the most common of trailering accidents.

Tires   Look for any extensive wear in any one spot. Something may be out of alignment. A blown tire could send your trailer out of control or even cause it to overturn. Make sure, too, that you have a spare that is in good condition.

Lights and Brakes   Hook these up and see that they are in good working order. As for the brakes, they are *very*

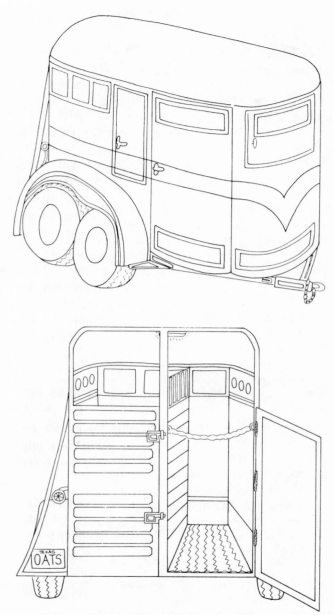

Two-horse tandem trailer.

important. Check to see what your state's traffic rules have to say about them and then "stick to the rule."

Safety Chains, Hitch, and Door Latches   Rust and corrosive wear are the villains here. If the rust has not gone too far, a good paint job will save the day.

Center Divider   Many horsemen prefer the type of divider that is not solid. This is because many horses are "climbers" and need to spread their feet into the other stall in order to feel secure. Great! What about the horse in the other stall? I have seen too many horses badly injured in this way to want to have anything else than a *solid* center divider.

Climbers are made, not born. They are the result of the human being up front doing a poor job of driving, so that the horse must scramble all over the walls in order to stay upright. If you find yourself with a horse that is a climber, take him for a few short hauls while driving with utmost care. You may just convince him he can get along very well with only his own stall to stand in.

Wheel Bearings, etc.   This includes all of those mechanical odds and ends that I freely admit I do not understand. *If* the trailer has passed your inspection up to this point, it is probably worth pouring $25 to $30 into it for a complete mechanical inspection by your favorite service station or garage.

And, while you are en route, have someone else drive while you play horse and ride in the back. Check for adequate ventilation, both while moving and while standing for several minutes. Notice if there are any excessive noises or rattles that might put your horse's nerves in a dither. And, most important, notice if any exhaust fumes are being sucked up into the trailer compartment from the tow car.

IMPORTANT EXTRAS

Like cars, trailers come both as stripped models and with almost every luxury but a built-in groom. However, some of these luxuries I consider to be essential, and I would hope that you find your dream trailer with them included.

Escape Doors It is hard to believe that a trailer would be designed and made without an escape door, but I have seen them. Now, regardless of what they are called, an escape door is not intended to provide an escape for you after you have walked into the trailer with your horse behind you. (I cannot think of a quicker way to collect your hospitalization. *Never load a horse in this manner.*) That door is intended to give you access to your horse's head to tie him and release him, as well as give him food and water. In fact, on many trailers there are only "feed doors," and you would have to be a starving midget to exit through them.

Interior Lighting Horses hate the dark, and if you have ever tried to load a horse at night you will know what I am talking about. A dome light will save you countless frustrating hours of trying to load your horse when the show has gone over into the evening hours and you find you have parked yourself in the darkest corner of the parking lot. Also it will give you a sense of assurance when you glance into the mirror while driving at night and note that all are riding well and comfortably.

Tack Compartment A tack compartment is not only handy; it helps you to avoid stowing all that heavy equipment in the trunk of your car, thus putting weight in the towing vehicle, where it is least needed.

Hitching Rings These are welded-on steel rings at various points on the outside of the trailer. Hitching rings will allow you to tie your horse in safety when you are stopped for a rest or at your destination. Several rings located in the head area will allow you to tie your horse as you desire. As for securing your horse for travel, I find that if I cross-tie my horse he rides with more comfort and a sense of security. And *never* use anything other than safety-release snaps to "tie" your horse in a trailer.

Floor Mats These are not a standard item in most cases. They may or may not come with a used trailer. If you are lucky enough to inherit a pair, clean them and check for any worn spots. And always, after every trip, remove and wash them and do not return them until both they and the floor have had sufficient time to dry.

If you find you don't have them you will have to provide them. Your horse *must* have firm footing on which to ride. They may be ordered through companies listed in any horse magazine, or you can make your own for about one-tenth the price. Go to a tire recapper and buy some treads that are being discarded owing to flaws. They come in lengths of twelve feet, so you can get two strips out of each section. Lay these strips side by side in the bottom of the trailer, making sure they fit securely with no overlapping or gaps in which an errant foot could become entangled. A good-quality tread should be heavy enough to stay put yet be easy to remove for cleaning after each trip.

Tailgates   The type of ramp or tailgate is a matter of your horse's choice rather than yours. Some horses will simply not walk up a ramp. I guess it seems insecure, and it may be. Others will not take that first giant step up into the trailer bed.

If you do decide that a step-up trailer is the mode of transportation you prefer, let me give you a word of caution: choose the type with a tailgate that closes with latches rather than the bar that swings down from the center post. I am now going to elucidate another one of those safety factors—the last time, I promise.

On some trailers there is a bar that swings into place from a center post to hold the door shut. It is all too easy for this bar by accident to be left protruding into the empty door opening. I was witness to a horrifying accident that cost the life of a lovely young Arabian mare, who was in line that day for a championship. She was a nervous traveler and always backed out quickly from the trailer. This day someone untied her and did not have a good enough hold on her head to steady her exit. When she backed out she caught her leg on the protruding latch bar and literally tore the leg off. She had to be destroyed immediately—putting an end to an out-standing show career and breaking the heart of her twelve-year-old owner.

Hence, should you buy a step-up trailer, be sure to get one with the bolts on the doors themselves. There is no use taking any more chances than you need to. Perhaps someday they will discontinue the other type of latch.

Perhaps, too, this might be a good place to remind you *always* to release your horse's head and *attach* his lead shank *before* you open the tailgate or undo that butt chain. It is entirely possible that this was one of the factors involved in the accident just mentioned.

CLEAN AND POLISH IT

Once you have signed the check and your receipt is in hand, take your beautiful trailer home and do a little reconditioning before you take your horse for his first spin.

Clean it out thoroughly, removing any old hay or grain left in the feeding compartment. Give it a good wash job and take it to the service station to be lubed and have the tire pressure checked.

If it needs painting, have it done. Even the $29.95 special will do. Unpainted metal will rust and you know what rust will do to the strength of metal. Besides, this way you can have it painted to match your car or truck, and a matching rig is so ego uplifting.

IS YOUR CAR READY TO TOW?

Most cars are designed to haul passengers not horses. Pulling a heavy metal trailer plus one or two thousand-pound horses is not going to improve the engine behavior of most cars. It is best to talk over your car's hauling potential with someone knowledgeable, such as your garage attendant. Among other things that your car should be equipped with are heavy-duty springs and shocks, a large enough radiator to provide your engine with the proper cooling, and a strong, safe hitch.

If your trailer sits level it will tow better and your horse will not be fighting his footing. To accomplish this you can have your trailer supplied with a load leveler so that, no matter what the load, the car and trailer will ride level. If the hitch is too low it will make the horse ride head down, and the trailer and the car will drag on all the low spots. If it rides too high you could lose the trailer going over a bump.

PULLING A TRAILER

Now it's there, what do you do with it? Well, whatever you do with it, practice first. Plan to spend at least a couple of Saturdays driving around without your horse in order to achieve that I've-been-doing-this-for-years feeling, before you subject him to your braking and backing problems.

Pulling a trailer is simple (ha! ha!) if you but remember a few rules. Always drive as though you were pulling a long freight train. Be a defensive driver and plan ahead for the idiot who will pull out in front of you doing thirty-five when you are doing fifty-five. Keep your distance from other drivers and stay in the lane meant for trucks and trailers. When you do have to brake, do it gently, and when approaching a stoplight do it in a series of stops rather than one long one.

Take all corners as slowly and with as little quick movement as possible. Remember that your horse is not sitting —he is standing, and has no idea which way you are planning to turn or where you are heading.

As for backing a trailer, I still have problems. The basic rule is that for the trailer to go to the right you cramp the steering wheel to the left and vice versa. The problem is that if your car and the trailer are not absolutely straight and the wheels all in line before you begin this maneuver you are going to end up with a jack-knifed mess and a seasick horse. Frankly, I avoid backing at all costs, planning my entry and departure into shows and various meetings with all the strategy of the Second World War. I still recall in nightmarish detail the time I drove up a narrow dead-end lane and had to back my trailer three and a half miles with a green yearling playing games behind (or should I say in front?) of me. What it all boils down to is, if you don't have plenty of room, don't try to back, and try *not* to get caught in this type of situation.

DRESSED TO TRAVEL

Remember that your horse is not wearing a safety belt and that he has to stand in a swaying trailer while you ride in comfort up front. Thus he needs a little padding here and there to keep him bump-free during the ride.

One piece of equipment I would never let my horse travel without is a head bumper. This is a piece of felt, covered with leather, that looks like half a football helmet. They are relatively cheap and great insurance even if you trailer only occasionally. Most trailers are built rather low and it is all too easy for a horse to pull back and hit his head on the roof—and horses are rather sensitive up there.

Probably the most often injured area is the horse's legs. For this reason he really should have some kind of leg protection. Shipping boots are ideal, as they are quick to put on and you don't have to fuss with all those bandages and padding that constantly come undone or shift around. If you make your own (see Chapter 7) they are not expensive either.

Should you prefer to go the leg-bandage route, you can use either regular Ace bandages or buy a set of track bandages at the tack store; they come in pretty colors. Any

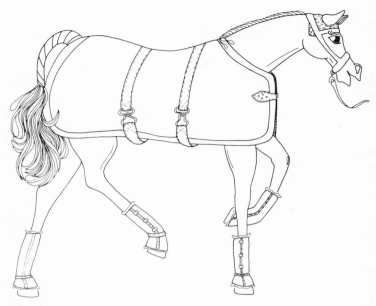

What the well-dressed horse wears for travel: sheet; head bumper; shipping boots and tail bandage.

number of things can be used as padding—cloth diapers, terrycloth hand towels, washable imitation sheepskin—just as long as it is washable and affords a cushioning effect under the bandage. But don't use cotton batting. You will have to throw it away each time, and that gets expensive after a while.

The bandage should cover the leg from below the knee and hock to below the coronet. Some people even give their horses added protection by putting bell boots on under the bandages, but if you pad the coronet area well I don't think that is necessary. The one problem with the use of bandages rather than shipping boots is that you must be careful not to wrap or tie them so tightly that circulation is lost.

To bandage the leg begin with the padding. Wrap it securely, around twice if it will go. Then, beginning at the middle of the cannon bone, wrap the bandage upward to the knee, then back down over the coronet area and up to the middle again. Fasten the bandage with a diaper pin and cover that with masking tape so that it won't come undone accidentally.

If your horse is a tail rubber, or you have braided the tail, you may wish to wrap it. Use a regular Ace bandage and wrap from the top down, beginning as high up as possible. Fasten it with a diaper pin on the outside.

Whether you sheet or blanket your horse depends upon him and the weather. Keep in mind that if the trailer is closed in it can become a sweat box in the summer. Even in the winter you may find that a sheet is equal to a blanket in his stall at home. On the other hand, the trailer may be drafty and you will want to compensate for this, especially if the weather is cold and rainy. I like to put a light sheet on my horse even in the summer in order to keep him clean on the way to wherever we are going. (See Chapter 7 on how to make your own summer sheet.)

A word of caution: *Never trailer a horse with his tack on him!* In my area I see a lot of working cowboys following this practice and it never ceases to amaze me that their horses do not get hung up in the trailer. May their luck always hold.

EVERYONE INTO THE TRAILER!

Unless you plan to trailer your horse only enough to get him to your home, where he will stay until you tire of him, I would hope that you paid attention in Chapter 1 and have bought a horse that is trailer-wise. Life is just too darned short to spend it fighting with a horse over whether or not he is going to accompany you to wherever you are going.

Furthermore, unless it is a professional trainer who is one of the sparring partners in these arguments, it is the horse that usually wins. If you are stuck with one of these long-term nonloaders my advice to you is either to call in a trainer to do the honors or to sell him!

If your horse is trailer-wise, keep him that way. When loading him try to park the trailer next to a fence or wall so that he has no choice but to follow the straight and narrow path between you on one side and the fence, or wall, on the other. Lead him quietly and with assurance, letting him sniff at the trailer before he enters it—even though it is his very own. And *never look back at him.* He is going to stop automatically, and once stopped he may be difficult to start up again.

Ideally a horse should walk up to the trailer with you, let you throw the lead over his back, and walk in without assistance while you fasten the butt chain, close the gate and walk calmly around to tie his head. It is not difficult to get your horse to this degree of trailering confidence if you start with one already accustomed to trailering.

To teach him to perform in this way, walk up to the trailer with him and get him to put one foot in, then throw the lead shank over his withers, give a little tug on the side of the halter, and at the same time give a voice command: "Get in," "Hop up," "Get moving." And when he finally does this right, praise him lavishly and have a tidbit for him. Do not try to accomplish this all in one day. Just work into it each time you go someplace, and one fine day you'll find he jumps in even without the command.

But perhaps your horse is just a little new to the whole situation and is merely leery, not downright antagonistic. With enough time, at least three or four weeks, and enough patience, you can show him the way to trailering happiness.

Begin by introducing the trailer to him as a part of his environment. Bring the trailer into his pasture, block it up securely, and tie the doors open if it is that type. Then begin to feed him his grain in the trailer, putting it first in the doorway, or on the ramp, and moving it farther into the trailer each day until he is happily munching it out of the feed box.

If your horse lives in a stall you will have to do the next best thing. Park the trailer where he can eye it whenever he looks out his door. Then feed him his grain in the same manner as above with you holding him on a lead.

Do not try to rush things. You will only set yourself back several days. In teaching a horse to load, the only way is with patience and perseverance. Keep in mind it is almost impossible to show a horse who is boss when you are on the ground and face to face. On that basis it is not so much brains that count as brawn, and brawn he has plenty of.

AWAY WE GO!

After you and your horse gain confidence in each other and you do not feel so intimidated by the contraption following your car's every move, you are going to want to start really traveling—to shows a day or so's ride away, an endurance ride, or just a trip to a national or state park. Once you get rolling, it is really quite easy. However, there are a few points to keep in mind to make sure that all rolls along smoothly.

If you plan to cross any state lines you should have a health certificate and VEE vaccination certificate. These you can obtain from your veterinarian. And in the Western states you will need a brand inspection certificate as well, even if your horse is not branded. (You get this from your local brand inspector. To obtain his name and address contact your local county office of the State University Extension Service.) Elsewhere you should carry some type of proof of ownership: a bill of sale or registration papers.

As for driving try to stick to the interstate highways. You will find the driving much smoother as well as make faster time. Also you will be able to plan your nightly stopovers well in advance. As for stopping to rest your horse, a good rule of thumb is every hundred miles. If you are traveling along a highway that has rest areas plan to make these your destinations. Pull in and park away from the other cars. If your horse loads and unloads easily (and he should by now) take him out of the trailer every three or four hours and let him walk around for about ten to fifteen minutes to get the stiffness out of his joints and possibly relieve himself. This is especially important if your horse is a gelding. Sometimes there is not room enough in the trailer for him to stretch out, and he will be extremely uncomfortable if you neglect to remember this. And, if he drops a little package at these way-side layovers, do be thoughtful and clean it up. A dustpan is handy for this.

Make sure that you have a water bucket that will fit through the feed door and offer him some each time you stop. Remember, too, that water changes in character from area to area. Buy a bottle of oil of wintergreen and begin adding a couple of drops to his water at home some days before your trip. Continue to do so as you travel—he'll think he never left home.

Keep him well supplied with hay to munch on as the miles roll by and you'll both have a good trip.

HORSE TALK

Butt chains   Rubber-covered chains, or ropes, which fasten behind the rump of the horse, thus preventing him from putting his weight on the tailgate.

Climber   A horse that tries to climb the wall while the trailer is in motion. Also called a scrambler.

Gooseneck trailer   A trailer with a forward extension that sits in the bed of a pickup truck. Because much of the weight is on the pickup in front of the rear axle, this kind of trailer is easier to maneuver and there is very little weaving.

Hock boots   Special boots made to fit over the horse's hocks to prevent them from being bruised by the tailgate.

In-line or shotgun trailer   A trailer designed so that the horses stand one behind the other. Because weight is not put on the towing car due to axle spread, these trailers are easier to pull.

Safety-release snaps Special ties made with snaps that will release even though there is pressure on them. Used to secure the horse in the trailer. They are *vital* to have in case of emergency.

Scrambler See CLIMBER.

Shipping boots Special boots made to protect the horse's legs while traveling.

Stock trailer A trailer with slatted sides, either open or closed and without dividers or feed box—used for hauling cattle, etc.

Tandem trailer Tandem refers to the axles. In a tandem trailer there are two, one right in front of the other.

7

Really Do-
It-Yourself

IF YOU CONSIDER your personal tool box to be well
equipped when its contents consist of a hammer and a
Phillips-head screwdriver, or after six weeks you have finally
mastered the art of threading your sewing machine, this
chapter is for you.

I know. I fit into both of the above categories. Not only
that, my budget does not always stretch far enough to pay
the prices asked for such ready-made items as summer
sheets and shipping boots, yet I am not about to go without
them. Thus the items to be found on the following pages
were somehow put together at one time or another by me
and have somehow managed to stay together long enough
so that I feel I can recommend them to you.

JUMPS

If you ride English and have access to even a microscopic
piece of vacant land, your first thoughts will probably be
toward a jump course all your own. But, if you have priced
ready-made standards, or even the brackets that go on
home-made standards, you may have blanched and given up
—especially if your talent with hammer and nails is a bit
on the weak side.

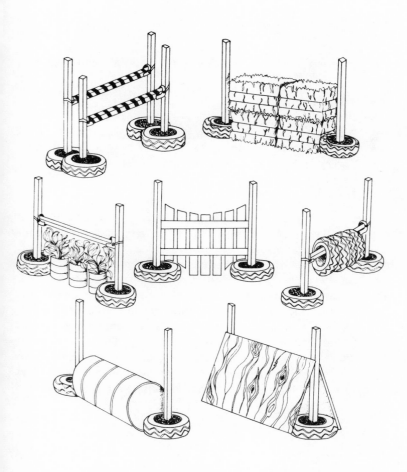

Take heart! *You* can build the seven-jump course shown here with a *minimum* amount of tools and talent. And it is guaranteed to withstand clumsy horses, people, and the elements for many a season.

Furthermore, it can be done for less than $40; for with the exception of the posts and cement for the standards and the crossbars, all the materials can be scrounged from such places as the county dump and friends' backyards. And you won't have to pound one nail.

Beginning with the standards, which are the same for all

the jumps, you will need the following materials and tools for each one:

- 4-by-4 fence post
- Old tire
- 2-pound coffee can
- 2 feet of heavy-gauge wire
- Enough cement mix to fill the tire center
- Small hatchet
- Tin snips

Place the tire on a level area of hard ground and fill the center with wet cement mix. Insert the end of the post into the center and allow the cement to harden. Measure the post at the points where you will want to attach the cup that holds the crossbar. Then, with the hatchet, make indentations of about one inch in depth at these points. Cut the coffee can with the tin snips to form a holder for the crossbar. Bend the wire into a loop. Punch holes in each side of the closed part of the can. Put the ends of the wire through to form a hanger, bending the wire flush to the inside. Hook this hanger into one of the indentations in the post and you now have one complete, sturdy standard—one that will stand up

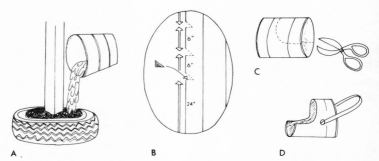

A, *fill center with cement and insert post;* B, *notch post as preferred, usually every six inches beginning one and a half to two feet from ground;* C, *cut coffee can to form holder;* D, *attach wire to can and hang on post.*

to a professionally made one right now. You will need two for each jump.

As for the jumps themselves, a little imagination and searching will give you a wealth of different types.

This is how I made mine.

To provide both height and spread I put two sets of standards one behind the other and added crossbars that I had painted with black and white strips for an even greater illusion of depth.

For a solid-looking jump that would equal the size and shape of a brick wall, I stacked up four bales of straw between two standards. Straw because it is lighter and will give way more easily than hay, is less costly, and will not tempt the horse to stop and chomp awhile.

The brush jump was made with one crossbar and some wooden nail keys planted with bushes I pulled up from the pasture. Surprisingly these are knocked over very little and I have had to replace the plants only a few times.

The gate was discovered in a neighbor's backyard, given a new coat of paint, and leaned against two standards.

If you have need for about 100,000 used tires, visit your county dump. I went wild and brought them home to use for just about everything. Strung on a bar they make an excellent jump.

Two discarded oil drums painted a bright color and laid end to end make a nice low jump. Add a crossbar and you can vary the height to suit yourself. My dump also has a rather healthy supply of these as well.

Two pieces of warped plywood became a chicken-coop jump. Just the right size and shape to be regulation.

REDECORATE HIS QUARTERS

If you took my advice and found an old bathtub or laundry tub for your steed's watering hole, don't just let it sit there naked; pretty it up.

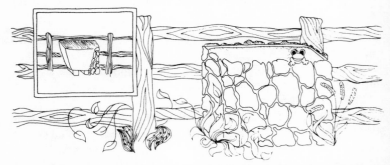

Set tub on cement blocks for drainage. Build stone facing using cement and field rocks.

An old-fashioned claw-footed tub is really picturesque in itself and needs only the addition of an interesting bit of painting—perhaps a flower or two with a butterfly thrown in, to set it off.

On the other hand, if it is basic ugly-modern, hide it! Make a foundation by setting each corner on a concrete block. This will get it off the ground and make drainage easier when you are cleaning it. Next build up a rock wall on all sides, using rocks you have picked up about your place and a sack of ready-mix cement. This rock wall will serve to keep the water cool in summertime, as well as make an attractive addition to your field.

For pasture dwellers it is always nice to have a place other than the ground to serve up hay. In my area almost every pasture housing cattle sports a low, sturdy feed box that is seemingly indestructible. When there were no beasties in sight one day, I climbed the fence and took a look to see how one was made. It certainly didn't appear to be too difficult a project. I went home, utilized some old lumber and had one whipped up in less than an hour.

You can probably find enough scraps at home or your lumber dealer's to do the same thing. You will need:

- Two pieces of 4-by-12 for the base—about 2 feet in length

- Six or seven 2-by-6-inch boards of whatever length you wish your feeder to be
- Enough 2-by-4-inch boards to make sides all the way around
- A handful of 3-inch nails. (Get the best quality available; cheap ones bend and are annoying to say the least.)

Set the two 4-by-12s on their sides and nail the 2-by-6 boards onto them to make a floor for the feeder. Position the base pieces so that they are about one-fourth of the way in from each end. Measure the 2-by-4 boards to make the sides, and nail on, making sure that *no nails* are protruding anywhere. If you don't own a saw, you can have the lumber sawed for you at the lumber yard for a small sum.

I made my feeder three years ago and it is still going strong, even after several "discussions" in and around it by my four-footed children.

Finding a strong place to tie up your horse can sometimes

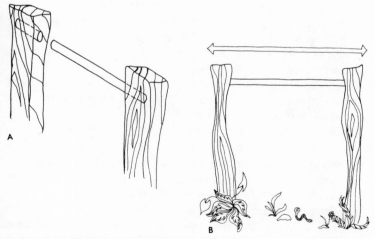

A, *drill holes in tops of two 4-by-4 fence posts and insert length of pipe;*
B, *bury posts in ground using some cement to hold them firmly in place.*

be a problem—but never at your own stable if you take the short time it takes to put up this easily made hitching post.

Begin with two 4-by-4 fence posts and a length of 2-inch galvanized pipe. Drill holes near the tops of the posts the size of the pipe. (If you don't own an electric drill, and you probably don't, borrow one. They are a snap to use and I found they were so much fun I bought one of my own to play with.) Insert the pipe into the holes and then plant the posts into holes in which you have dumped some wet cement mix. Once the cement dries you will have a hitching post that only God or a herd of termites can destroy.

REDECORATE YOUR QUARTERS

Make your tack room a sunny and pleasant place. Do a little interior decorating and I bet you'll want to keep it neat and tidy from then on—all the better for your tack and tools.

Begin with the basics. A handy saddle rack that folds up out of the way when not in use is easy to make. Take a piece of 2-by-4 about 2½ feet in length. Attach it to the wall with a strong gate hinge. Add a hook to the outer end and an eye where it meets the wall, so that you can hook it up when you don't need it.

Bridle and halter holders can be made by nailing one-pound coffee cans to the wall. Be sure to put them high enough so that the reins can hang freely.

Make a place to store your blankets, sheets, and saddle pads by installing a closet pole along one wall. There are brackets made just for this purpose that you can buy at the same place you got the closet pole. This way you will have no excuse for not airing those things properly.

For your grooming tools, a tack box is nice when you are off to a show, but at home it has a tendency to become jumbled if things are stored therein. Buy an attractive shoe bag and hang it on the wall. You will have a pocket for each

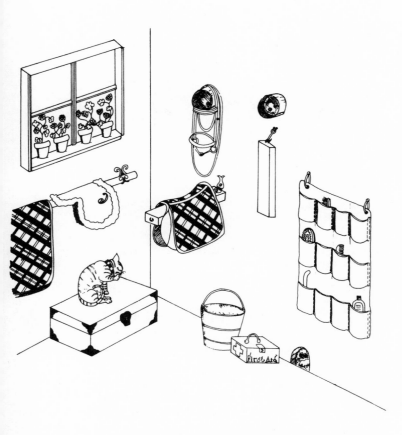

separate tool, and if you label the pockets you will know if something is missing.

Now paint everything a nice cheery color. This is a good idea for anything you take to a show as well. That way you will be able to spot it easily and claim ownership should a bucket or box go astray.

RECYCLE THOSE LEVI'S

Being an average American, I would presume you have now made your old jeans into just about everything imaginable; except perhaps the following.

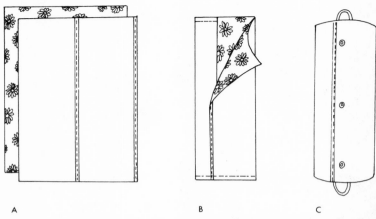

A, sew rectangles of jeans material and plastic lining right sides together, turn and hem; B, fold into envelope and sew seams; C, add snaps and D-rings.

Cantle Bag Cut off a portion of one leg, about 20 inches in length, and open it at the inner seam so that you have a rectangle. Cut a piece of plastic the same size for the lining. Sew these together, right sides together, and turn. Hem. Fold and sew as if you were making a clutch purse. Add some heavy-duty snaps to secure it shut and some D-rings on either end for securing it to the saddle. Stuff it with your lunch and away you go.

Feed Bag Cut about 20 inches off the widest part of one leg. Turn inside out and sew one end shut. Hem the other, making a wide double-fold hem for strength. Sew two ties about 2½ feet long to each side. To make the ties cut 2 pieces of jeans material about 3 inches wide and about 30 inches in length from the other leg. Fold each piece lengthwise with the right sides together and seam. Turn right side out and hem one end, then sew the other to the feed bag. Repeat this with the second tie. Fill with carrots and present it to your loved one.

Shipping Boots These are *very* expensive items and you can make a nifty set yourself, utilizing a pair of jeans and a yard of imitation fleece—washable, of course. Begin by

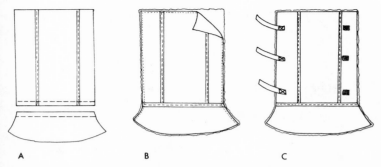

A, *cut pieces from jeans material as shown;* B, *sew together and line with fleece;* C, *add Velcro fasteners.*

cutting off the legs from a pair of jeans and opening up the outside seams. Make 4 rectangles about an inch longer than the length of your horse's cannon bone and 2 inches wider than it takes to go around. Cut 4 more pieces the same width and approximately 4 inches in length, with an apron effect on each side (see diagram). Sew these together into 4 single pieces. Cut a piece of fleece to match each jeans piece. Sew these together, right sides facing. Turn, hem and finish by sewing on tapes or Velcro fasteners on the jean material side.

A Boot Bag for You   Some people like to keep their expensive boots all nice and shiny by storing them in a boot bag. They may even carry them to the show in one. If you have an old pair of wide, bell-bottomed jeans the boot bags are quickly made. Cut off the bottoms of the jeans to the height you want, sew the bottoms together and hem the tops. Add some snaps along the inside seams to hold the two pieces together. To hang or carry the bag make a loop at the top, using one of the jean belt loops or a piece of twill tape. There you are, a boot bag just as snazzy as those at the tack shop.

Grooming Apron   To make this you will need a pair of overalls. If you are a teen, this should present no problem. If you are not, ask around or check the secondhand clothing stores for one. Remove the legs to the length you prefer, open up the front and rear middle seams and resew, just as if

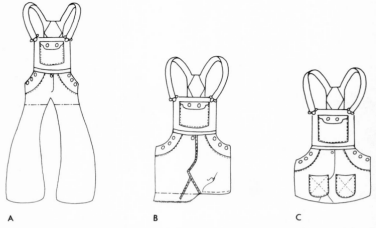

A, *cut legs from overalls and open crotch seams;* B, *sew front and back seams to form skirt, hem;* C, *remove pockets from back and any from legs, attach to front.*

you were making a jeans skirt. Remove the pockets from the rear, plus any that are on the cutoff legs, and sew them to the front of the apron. Start grooming.

NICE THINGS FOR YOUR HORSE

Fleece is soft and cuddly and will make your horse feel pampered. Washable imitation fleece can be used for making as many items as your imagination can come up with. It is easy to work with, doesn't ravel, is long-wearing and relatively inexpensive.

English saddle pads can be beautifully made from this material and will cost you just about half what a ready-made pad will. Cut two pieces the size you want, using your saddle for a pattern and cutting about two inches wider all the way around. With right sides together, sew with about a one-inch seam. Turn right side out and finish by hand. To keep the pad from getting out of shape, quilt it with long running stitches and heavy carpet thread. Add twill tape billet keepers.

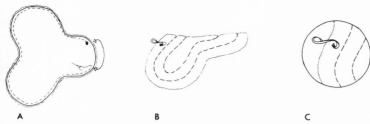

A, *cut two pieces the shape of your saddle*; sew right sides together, turn and hem by hand; B, *quilt with long, running stitches*; C, *add tape billet keepers*.

Western blankets can be made in the same manner. If you want to make them a little thicker add a layer of sheet foam rubber inside. You might try designing some interesting patterns, using various colors of fleece.

Use the leftover pieces to make nose rolls, curb strap covers, and girth covers.

Have fun. Dare to be different. Be the first one on your block to sport a baby-blue saddle pad with matching girth and nose roll. (But remember to keep it in the neighborhood —not at the show.)

SUMMERTIME IS SHOW TIME

It's only natural to want to dress up your horse to go to the show. And, of course, you want him to stay clean. But sometimes ready-made sheets can be a little warm in the summer, especially in closed trailers. The answer, then, is to tailor-make your horse his own sheet in a cooler fabric.

First make a pattern from your present sheet or blanket to see how much yardage you will need. Then search the drapery section of your yardage store for an inexpensive, loosely woven, yet *strong* fabric that will make a fashionable-looking show sheet. Plaids are nice or you might try a colored burlap. Do buy material that can easily be cleaned; and do not buy any material that is held together mainly with a heavy coat of sizing. This will be itchy on your horse and your sheet will begin to dissolve as soon as your horse starts to sweat.

Purchase some wide twill tape to match—enough to bind the outside edges completely plus a reinforcement strip down the middle of the back. In the notion section you should be able to find belt webbing and buckles. Buy enough to make two surcingles and a front closure. When sewing your sheet, use heavy-duty thread and sew each seam twice.

A cooler, if you want to be really snazzy, can be whipped up in no time for about $10. Watch for the sales or visit your dime store and purchase a loosely-woven queen-size bed spread. Be sure the material is worthy of your horse and will not disintegrate should you catch it on a nearby thorn bush. Trim the spread to fit your horse and bind the outside edges

Make a handsome but inexpensive cooler quickly by edging a bedspread with tape and adding ties.

with matching drill or cotton tape. Attach two ties, using the same tape, and you are ready to cool your horse in style.

MAKING IT PAY

By now I am sure you have realized that almost any one of the above items, made in quantities by you, might just be the ticket to keeping your horse supplied with his daily quota of alfalfa and oats.

For instance . . . how about offering saddle pads and matching rolls in a variety of colors not found at the tack shop, or made-to-order show sheets, or sheets and matching shipping boots of colored denim? Or you might just while away the time between show classes macraméing lead ropes or split-eared bridles. Put your mind to work. I'll bet you can come up with something different that everyone will be begging you to supply them with.

As an example I feel I must tell you a true story about a friend of mine. Like you and me, she is not too swift in the do-it-yourself field, yet she came up with an idea that has earned her enough money to have a four-stall stable built, buy two more horses, and keep her nags in healthy amounts of food from now until forever.

Here in northern California we are troubled with face flies. This variety of pest is not content to bother the horse just around his eyes, and the usual type of fly mask thus gives him very little protection. To solve this problem she took a section of nylon window screening and cut a piece to cover the front of her horse's head. She made darts at the sides so the areas over the eyes pouched out, and then she bound the whole affair with wide colorful cotton seam tape. She then cut pieces of inch-wide elastic and sewed them so that they fit under the chin and jowls and over the poll.

This mask worked so beautifully that everyone who saw it wanted one. Soon she was in business. The feed stores got into the act as well, buying them from her wholesale; and a friend who was a traveling salesman carried them up and down the state for her. The last time I heard, she was considering putting a patent on the idea. From such, moderate wealth is born. And, believe me, if she can do it so can you.

8

Grooming That Shows

THEORETICALLY grooming should be an everyday job—at least during the riding season—and a job well done if it is to count at all. But today's horse owner may just be so busy earning his horse's keep that he barely has time to ride, let alone groom. Thus grooming sometimes consists of taking a swipe at the worst dirt and cleaning out the feet. O.K., I'll go along with that, and it probably won't hurt your horse any if he spends his days out in a pasture, where he has plenty of room to roll and get his circulation moving. If, however, he spends his days in a stall, a little more effort should be made, for the purpose of grooming is not just to get the dirt out. Grooming gets the horse's circulation going, helps to distribute the oil from his glands onto his coat, and helps keep up his muscle tone. It also gives you a chance to check him over for any strange lumps or bumps and to get to know him just a little better.

If you want to do any showing you must plan on a *complete daily grooming,* beginning at least six to eight weeks in advance of the first show and continuing throughout the show season. It really takes that long to get the extra bloom on a horse that will put him favorably in the judge's eye. I must admit that, at times, I have taken a horse straight out of winter pasture, spent four or five hours on him, and taken him to a show the following day—but certainly not with the intent of entering a halter class. And rarely has a horse with that type of treatment ever figured in the top of the class. I just men-

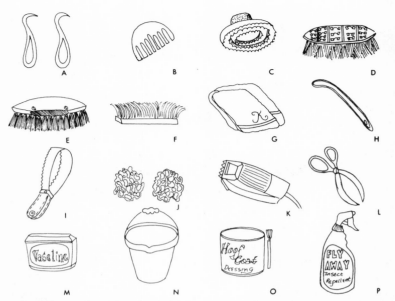

Grooming equipment. A, *hoof pick;* B, *mane comb;* C, *rubber curry comb;* D, *dandy brush;* E, *body brush;* F, *water brush;* G, *towels or stable rubbers;* H, *sweat scraper;* I, *shedding blade*; J, *sponges;* K, *clippers;* L, *strong shears;* M, *Vaseline;* N, *bucket;* O, *hoof dressing;* P, *insect repellent.*

tion it to let you know that it can be done, but only if what you are doing is using the show as schooling for your horse.

BASIC GROOMING

Proper grooming is a time-consuming task and a hard one. You should be relatively tired by the time you finish. No doubt you know the correct way to groom, but let us go over the basic procedure just in case you are missing a step somewhere along the way.

Naturally you must have the basic tools with which to work. You will need the following:

- Hoof pick. Buy two. One will always be missing and, anyway, you should always carry one in your pocket for problems along the trail.

- Mane and tail comb. If you are planning on doing any braiding.
- Rubber currycomb. Metal ones are rather rough on a horse's tender skin, and if you use one you will be tempted to really dig in when there is a big clot of mud on him.
- Hard dandy brush. The type with bristles that looks like a broom.
- Soft dandy brush. The type with soft white bristles (a body brush will do as well but somehow a dandy brush is easier to work with and lasts longer).
- Water brush. A dime-store scrub brush works well, or use an old dandy brush. This is to use when you are working with his mane and tail.
- Old towels. Linen stable rubbers are nice if you are a millionaire, but I'll bet you have more old towels than money to throw around.
- Sweat scraper. You'll find you use this more than you think.
- Shedding blade. Nothing takes its place during the spring months.
- Sponges. Two. Break down and buy the natural ones, which will outlast the plastic variety ten to one.
- Bucket. More than one if you can afford them.
- Strong scissors. Don't get the ones with the pointed ends.
- Small-animal clippers. Get the best quality you can, for anything less is a waste of money, but, unless you really want to go into the clipping business, don't bother buying expensive body clippers (explanation later).
- Hoof dressing. Either a commercial or homemade one.
- Insect repellent. For spring and summer use.
- Vaseline or cod liver oil. To stimulate hair growth on old cuts and wounds by softening the skin and protecting the new hair growth. Probably this belongs in the old wives' tale department, but I, and many others I know, swear by it. Anyway it can't hurt.

Begin your daily chore by cross-tying your horse. This way he won't always be moving away from you and you have a better idea of what is happening at the biting end.

Begin by picking out his feet so you won't forget to do it later and leave something the size of Mt. Hood jammed into his shoe. Always be sure to clean out the cleft along the sides of the frog and take a sniff while you are there to catch any first signs of thrush.

Now, with your currycomb in your right hand and stiff dandy brush in your left, begin at the poll and work your way to the other end. Use a circular rubbing action with the currycomb and follow it with short strokes of the dandy brush to bring up the dirt that the currycomb loosened. Clean your brush against the currycomb about every ten strokes and then tap the currycomb against your heel to knock out the dirt. Now do the other side.

Do not use the currycomb below the knees and hocks or on the head, no matter how much mud is there. Use the stiff dandy for his legs and for brushing out his mane and tail. (The mane and tail comb should be used as a tool only when braiding.)

Now take your soft dandy brush and go over his face and body. Repeat with a clean towel to smooth his coat thoroughly and distribute the oils. Wipe his eyes and nostrils with a damp sponge. Then, with a different sponge, clean the area under his tail.

Once or twice a week apply a hoof dressing both on the wall and the sole of the hoof. If you're counting pennies you can make an inexpensive dressing at home. Buy some regular glycerine at the drugstore and mix it in a ratio of one part glycerine to three parts water. Shake well each time before you use it. Buy a cheap paint brush with which to apply it.

Your horse's mane should lie to the off side (except on a roping horse), especially if your horse goes English. Some judges are pretty picky about this point. If it is lying on the near side or some cowlick is misbehaving, you might finish up your grooming by dampening the mane with your water brush and putting it where you want it. If you have the time you might even braid it occasionally and leave the braids in overnight—no longer if your horse lives in a pasture, as he is sure to find some spot and rub them out, removing a goodly portion of mane as well. This is a good time to practice your braiding if you are not proficient at that chore.

Some horses, and it always seems to be the light-colored ones, insist on prettying themselves up with assorted manure and grass stains. These are best taken care of as they occur. Manure stains can be removed with a little soap and water but grass stains are a bit tougher. Some bran rubbed into the spot and then brushed out will sometimes (not always) do the trick.

If your horse has any bald spots resulting from a recent injury you might smear a little Vaseline or cod liver oil on them. It not only protects the new hairs growing in but softens the skin, preventing permanent baldness.

Whether you are performing a complete grooming before you ride or not, there are always a couple of things you should do before putting your horse away. Always rub him dry on any areas that are sweaty, such as underneath the saddle and between his front legs. Then brush him so that no sweat is left in to dull his coat. If it is warm weather these areas can be rinsed off with a large sponge and any excess water removed with a sweat scraper. Or, if it is warm enough, you might rinse him off completely. Just be sure that he is dry before you put him up. If you are blanketing him, put his blanket on and then push handfuls of clean straw up underneath, along his back. This lets the damp areas dry out completely.

In the spring a part of your daily grooming will include the use of a shedding blade. Your horse is probably kind of itchy and should enjoy this; just don't get carried away and take part of his skin along with the loose hair. And go gently on areas like his belly and places where a bone is close to the

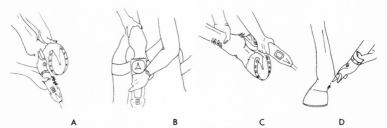

A, *clean the hair from the pastern by clipping upward over the coronary band;* B, *clip the front of the leg, also using the upward motion;* C, *trim the fetlock, taking care not to cut the ergot;* D, *blend the clipped and unclipped portions by using a downward feathering motion.*

surface. If your horse is not shedding out as much as you think he should, you might check him for worms. A worm-infested horse will retain his winter coat much longer than a worm-free one will.

CLIPPING

Show season and the shedding out of your horse do not always coincide; in fact, they hardly ever do. But, unless your horse resembles something from the ice age, I would strongly advise against giving him a complete body clip. In the first place you must be prepared to replace his natural blanket with one or more that you buy, and you must keep a constant eye on the weather so that he doesn't come down with a case of the sniffles. Secondly, a horse that has been clipped out never does achieve the smooth, satiny look of one that has been allowed to shed out naturally. Try sprucing him up by clipping (booting) his lower legs and getting rid of the excess hair on his face first, and see if that isn't enough to get by with for those first few shows.

A complete clipping with large horse clippers is not a job to be taken lightly. It takes real expertise. I would suggest that you have your nearby stable do it for you. Most stables will do the job for about $20 to $25. If you think this is too high a price you should realize that it can take two to three hours to do; besides, a lot of people, even experts, have been pretty badly hurt by an uncooperative horse. Plan to have it done long enough in advance, a week or two, so that the coat will have a chance to even up and get rid of any "railroad tracks" left by the clippers.

Small clipping jobs, on the other hand, should be manageable by almost anyone. These jobs include doing the legs, removing excess hair around the head and the bridle path, and even roaching the mane. Small animal clippers are fine for this.

If you have never worked around your horse with clippers, a word of warning is in order. The hearing of a horse is quite acute, and the clippers must sound to him as if he is being attacked by a jet fighter. He may, therefore, react violently if you walk up to him without warning, snap on the clippers, and immediately try to clip his mane. There are ways to overcome this problem. One way is to leave the clippers running at some distance while you groom him for a few days, introducing them gradually by moving them closer each day.

I know of cowboys who will say this is silly and will go ahead and twitch a horse and let him fight it out. Great! I know a lot of cowboys who are minus their front teeth, too. I say, why make a fighter out of your horse? Take your time, respect him, and in the end you will have a horse that will barely move an ear the next time you clip him.

You might begin by clipping his legs—maybe just one the first day. Begin with the hair around the coronet, then go up behind the back of the pastern and the fetlock. Try to keep the pressure as even as possible, overlapping as you go. Do not go above the knees and hocks. Use some downward strokes as you approach the area, blending the clipped portion in with the unclipped hair.

Whether you are doing a bridle path or roaching the entire mane, approach the clipping the same way. Starting at the poll, clip first one side, then the other, and then a strip down the middle.

A, *trim the mane by clipping the sides first and then finishing with one smooth path down the middle;* B, *pinch the ear together and trim the protruding hairs with a downward motion;* C, *clip the underjaw with an upward motion, pulling the skin taut with the other hand as shown.*

Three or four inches is a good length of bridle path for the English horse. On the Western horse the length of bridle path is a matter of looks. Some horses look better with longer ones rather than shorter. You might experiment by pushing a part of the mane to the other side of the neck and judging it for yourself before you go ahead and clip. The length of the mane is important if you are doing this, so it is best to do your mane pulling (more about that later) before you clip.

If your horse is a Westerner you might even consider roaching his mane. Horses with thick necks look better in this style, and if your horse has a mane that is not a thing of beauty this could be the answer. Just be sure before you make this decision; it takes a long time to grow out.

Now trim away any long hairs from around his chin and jaw. The feeler hairs, not his eyelashes, around his eyes are best cut with the scissors.

As to the hair in his ears, this is up to you. Perfectionists insist that they be clipped clean. To do this fold the ear back and clip downward against the growth of the hair. As stated earlier, most horses do not like the sound of the clippers and may jump about when they are in his ear, making it all too easy to give him a nasty cut or two. Then you are going to have a horse that will not be trusting of those clippers on any point of his anatomy.

In clipping the ears clean you remove the horse's protection against flies. Personally I think more of my horse's comfort than the opinion of a few judges, and most judges would not put down a horse that is otherwise impeccably groomed. Do cut the longer hairs that protrude from the ears, though. To do this fold the ear together and clip any hairs that are sticking out.

Watch your clippers to see that they don't become too hot. It is a good idea to dunk the head in a can of kerosene occasionally to clean out the hair and to cool the head.

Some horses never will learn to tolerate clippers. I have owned a few, and I have a friend who successfully shows her paint mare nationally and does all her clipping with a pair of scissors.

To do the legs with scissors cut the area around the coronet so that it has a nice even line. Then clip the fetlocks, shearing them vertically. If you clip them horizontally they will have a chopped appearance. Be careful not to cut the ergot, that horny protuberance, in your enthusiasm.

Trim the whiskers and the long hair underneath the chin. Again follow a vertical line along the jaw to avoid a chopped look. When doing the bridle path with scissors do not try to get too close, as a smooth look is almost impossible to achieve if you do. A quarter of an inch is a good length. Go with the line of the neck and follow the same procedure you would if you were clipping.

MANES AND TAILS

How your horse will wear his mane and tail depends a great deal on his occupation in life. If his is a glamour job, such as strutting his stuff in a Tennessee Walking Horse or Arabian Park Pleasure class, he will wear both his mane and tail long and full.

Though horsehair looks tough it is surprising how easily

it breaks when you don't want it to. Instead of brushing or
combing it you must pick it out each day, separating the hairs
carefully. Then finish the job by smoothing it with your hand.
This will add oil and make it shine. Some trainers keep the
tails in bags—kind of like horse hairnets. I don't think you
want to go this far, but that is how some of those long
glorious tails get that way.

On the other end of the scale, working stock horses wear
their tails short; pulled and thinned so that they fall just
short of the hocks. Roached manes and those that are pulled
so that they are only three or four inches long help to keep
the reins and ropes from tangling in the mane when the cowboy is working. The shortness of the tail is to keep it free from
burs and brush. The short mane and tail are also more flattering to the muscular build of the stock horse.

Hunters and jumpers also have their manes and tails pulled.
The tail is pulled so that it comes evenly to his hocks. If
the mane is to be braided during showing and at such events
as the opening of hunt season, it is best pulled to a length of
three inches and thinned enough to permit neat braids.

Pulling

This is a job that is both time-consuming and a bit hard on
the hands, so plan on doing it over a period of several days
and wear gloves while you are doing it.

To pull the mane, begin at the poll with a small hunk of hair
and "tease" it with the mane comb. Wrap the long hairs that
remain—three or four at a time—around your fingers or comb,
and pull them. I know horses are not supposed to have feeling
in the mane area but try pulling for a while and I think you will
note a definite reaction. Therefore, do not stay in one area
too long. Rather, continue down the length of the mane and
then start over again. This will also keep you from pulling too
much from one section and ending up with an uneven
appearance.

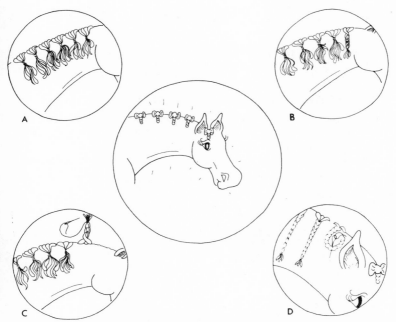

Braiding the mane. A, *separate the mane into one-inch sections;* B, *braid;* C, *secure the end by sewing with heavy thread;* D, *to make knobs, coil and sew until top of mane is reached, secure.*

Braiding the Mane

Sewing is the *only* way! If you use rubber bands you will find the braids do not lie flat and have a tendency to come undone at the worst possible times, usually in class.

Do not try to learn this art the day of the show. Give yourself several practice sessions when you have plenty of time and patience. Even when you are a pro, do the braiding the night before the show. There are too many other problems to confront you the day of the show, and if done right the braids should stay put until you undo them.

You will need a tapestry or yarn needle, heavy upholstery thread the color of your horse's mane, a bucket of water, your water brush, and a mane comb.

Begin by brushing the entire mane until it is completely free of tangles. Starting at the poll take a section approximately one to one and a half inches wide and dampen it. Plait this *tightly,* always starting your braid the same way each time. When you reach the end of the pigtail take your needle and about twenty inches of thread—which has been knotted and placed where you can get it easily, preferably not between your teeth—and stitch through the end of the braid.

At this point you must decide whether you want a balled effect, called a "nob," or a loop, called a "doorknocker." Nobs make a neater appearance and stay in place a lot longer, but they are a little more work to make. If you prefer a doorknocker you have merely to loop the braid up under itself and sew it securely to the top of the braid. To make a nob, roll the braid toward the base of the mane, sewing through at each turn and securing snugly on the final turn.

Continue on down the mane in this manner, being sure to leave about three or four inches of undone mane at the withers. This is to avoid having a braid underneath your saddle. The forelock is done in one braid. The plaits should feel hard and tight. Any that are soft and squashy must be undone and done again.

To put all the little stray hairs in place, squirt some hair spray on the finished job. I am against the use of aerosol sprays: they can scare the living daylights out of some horses.

A horse with a long skinny neck looks better with fatter braids, while those with short necks will look more handsome with a lot of little ones. In some places it is a custom to put ribbons on the plaits of jumpers and leave the hunters unadorned. It has always been my contention that anything done in the horse world is better if it is done in a simple, tasteful manner. I would thus eschew the use of ribbons. It is up to you. Just don't do it if you are showing your horse in a hunter class.

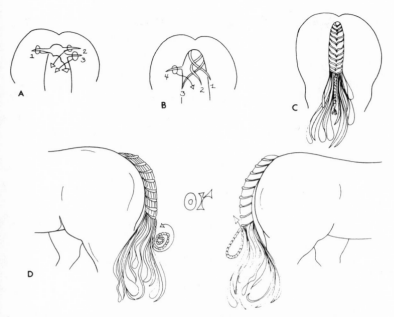

Braiding the tail. A, take a strand from one side and two from the other, twist these together in the center to begin your braid; B, plait, adding a strand from each side as you continue to braid; C, upon reaching the end of the tailbone introduce the end of your thread and continue to braid without adding any more hair. Complete braid and sew the end; D, finish with either a coil or a loop.

Braiding the Tail

This takes a little more skill, and some people never do seem to manage it properly. But there is no reason for you to be one of these people. The following method is my favorite and produces a nice braid.

Again, begin with a tangle-free tail. This is important. Now dampen the tail completely. Take three strands from under the base of the tail, beginning as high up as you can, two from one side and one from the other. Cross the strands in the center and begin braiding, adding a little from each side every time you cross over. The secret of a good tail braid is to take only a few strands of hair at a time and keep the braid as *tight* as possible all the way down. Braid in this manner until you reach just past the end of the tail bone. Now take about a forty-inch length of thread, introduce the end of it into the braid and continue plaiting without adding any more hair from the sides. Secure the end of this pigtail by sewing through it several times. You may now finish the braid in two different ways: by merely looping it under itself or by rolling it into a coil. Either way, sew it until you think it is never going to come undone.

BATHING

Bathing should *never* be done in any but the warmest of weather and even then as infrequently as possible. Bathing never replaces good grooming and should not be done any less than one week prior to a show—unless your horse takes a lovely roll in a mud puddle. It really takes that long to replace the natural oils in his coat.

A bath is best accomplished with a hose. This insures that you will get all that dulling soap out of his coat. If you are not sure how your horse will react around a hose you should approach him first with one that is dry, letting him sniff at it and casually playing it about his body so he may get used to it before you turn the water on.

Wet him down and apply a nondrying shampoo. You may buy an expensive one made especially for horses or do as I do. I buy an inexpensive human variety by the half gallon at my nearby discount house. Take your water brush and give him a good scrubbing, paying special attention to getting at the dandruff in the base of his mane and tail. Now rinse him off thoroughly. If you have resorted to pails of water, don't stint; any shampoo remaining will dry and make him appear in need of a dandruff cure. Now use your sweat scraper and get all the excess water out of his coat, scraping with the lay of the hair. Walk him until he is dry.

I am sure this advice is superfluous, but do give him his bath either on cement or in a grassy area. Dirt makes good mud awfully fast.

THE DAY BEFORE THE SHOW

This is the time to get all the equipment ready that you will be taking to the show. All of my life I have drooled over those beautiful and expensive tack boxes that are shown in the horse catalogs, but somehow my bank book has never given me a chance to buy one. I have had to make do with a nice, dull metal foot locker—a good sturdy one can be got at any army and navy surplus store. They are the right size to hold all of the following:

- Water pail. Horse shows are good places for germs, and the best place to find germs is in the communal watering hole.
- Extra halter and lead. It will be no time to look for one to borrow should yours break during one of those moments of excitement that occur at every show.
- Brushes. Both the soft and hard dandy ones. Your grooming should be complete, but he may step in some mud, so you might need the hard dandy brush; and you will want to give him a final spiffing up, so you will need the soft one.
- Currycomb. For the same mud puddle mentioned above.
- Hoof pick. Never be without one, no matter where you are.
- Four clean towels. More if you can find room. They are good for everything.
- Sponges. To wipe his eyes and nose just before class time and for cleaning the mustard off your shirt from that lunchtime hot dog.

- Scissors. For last-minute stray hairs, and threads on your coat.
- Sweat scraper. Just in case.
- Shoe polish. Only if you elect to polish his feet.
- Extra reins and girth. If you have them they are a great insurance policy. . . . May you never need them!
- Safety pins. Also for insurance.
- Insect repellent. His and yours.
- Band-Aids. For you: you don't want to bleed all over your clean horse should you be so clumsy as to cut yourself.
- Extra hair net. For you if you are a girl.
- Anything else you think you *might* need. It is a long way home and probably a long way to the nearest store.

That night groom your horse until he gleams, touch up any clipped area that needs it and braid his mane and tail if that is part of his beauty treatment. Cover the tail braid with a bandage. Put his blanket on and let him rest. This is no time for last-minute training.

THE DAY OF THE SHOW

Double check all your equipment. It is a good idea to have a check list; everyone gets rattled about this time, especially if it is 6 A.M. and you haven't had your coffee yet. Look at all those braids and take a peek under the tail bandage to make sure all is in order . . . ditto his blanket. Load everything, including him, and be on your way.

After you have unloaded him and checked yourself in, give him a drink and a little hay, and get that last-minute spiffing-up done. Give him a good going-over with your soft dandy brush and towel. Clean his eyes and nostrils. Pay particular attention to his hoofs. They should be clean and shining. A bit of steel wool will help give him a finished look, and if you are of the school to apply shoe polish do so at this time. Professional trainers don't go in for this practice much, but it is an individual thing and there is nothing wrong with it. Of course you are not going to do it if your horse's feet aren't naturally dark.

Just before you enter the show ring apply a little bug repellent to both him and you. Make sure it is not the type that has an oil base; give your horse about three minutes in a dusty ring with this on and he will look as if he has just spent half a day climbing out of the Grand Canyon.

There is a lot of money made nowadays on the sale of special show sprays to give your horse that "extra sparkle." You know the old saying about gilding the lily. If your horse is clean, healthy, and well groomed it *will show*. Take my word for it.

Now relax, enjoy yourself, and go buy a hot dog.

HORSE TALK

Banged tail   The style of tail worn by the English hunter, with the end of the tail pulled so that it is even with the point of the hocks.

Bloom   Good weight with a shiny, healthy-looking coat.

Bridle path   The patch behind the horse's ears and at the poll that is clipped clean for the crownpiece of the bridle.

Cross-tie   The proper way to tie a horse when grooming him, with ropes snapped into the rings on either side of the halter and tied to posts or the sides of the stable alley.

Hunter clip   A clip used on hunters during the winter months. The body is clipped, leaving the hair on the legs, and sometimes the saddle area, for protection against the cold.

Mud tail   Braiding the tail in one large pigtail, which is then doubled up and secured to keep the tail from becoming soiled on a rainy day.

Roached mane   A completely clipped mane. Frequently done on working cow horses so that the ropes will not become entangled.

Trace clip   A clip given to hunters in the winter. Partial areas of the neck, chest, belly, and buttocks are clipped. This gives the horse the warmth of his own coat but does away with the long hair where he has a tendency to sweat.

9

Dressing
the Part

SHOWING IS expensive. Terrific fun and a great sport, but it *is* expensive and therefore you don't want to make any mistakes.

It is not difficult to spend upward of $200 or $300 for one good show outfit. Take a trip to your nearest tack shop, ask them to outfit you correctly for the type of showing you plan to do, and see how fast the total mounts up.

But if you don't have $200 or $300 to spend on one outfit—and it doesn't stop there—or you simply don't want to, there are still ways you can come out looking like a winner.

The easiest way is to buy someone else's used outfit and have it altered. In addition to saving money you won't have that "brand new to the game" look. Even buying one or two of the more costly pieces secondhand can help. Check the bulletin boards at your local riding school, stable, or feed store for hunt caps, hunt coats, boots, chaps, or Western hats. Then complete your outfit with a trip to the tack shop.

Another way is to make some of those items that cost so much in the store yet can be sewn at home for about one-tenth the cost and without any great skill required. These include English hunt coats and vests and equitation suits for the Western rider.

LOOK BEFORE YOU BUY

Whatever you choose you must be very careful to *conform* to what they are wearing in your area, down to the last button on your sleeve. Take in a few shows, note what people wear and try to duplicate that look. The show ring is no place to "do your own thing." You will indeed look "outstanding" if you try to look different, but it will be the wrong kind of outstanding.

Fashions in the show world are pretty standard throughout the country, and they do not change from year to year, nor from area to area, so you needn't worry about having to throw out last year's look. The items that will differ will be small ones—ties, hat brims, barrettes. It is these things you look for. The most outstanding characteristic of a group of riders showing in a class is that they resemble a matched drill team, they are dressed so alike. The idea, then, is to *conform,* but then to go the others one better by your choice of fabric, color, texture; and to be *neater* than any of the others. There is a phrase in every horse-show rule book in the country, "Neatness to count," and although it is meant to apply to tack, you had better believe it applies to the rider as well. *Conformity* and *neatness* are the keys to remember when making your purchases.

WESTERN

Most rule books state that you must wear boots, a hat, and a long-sleeved shirt, and that chaps are optional. Oh that it were so simple! Let us start from the beginning.

What color is your horse—not your hair or eyes or complexion—your horse? The horse is the first thing the judge is going to see when you arrive in the ring, and the idea is to

This is an example of what a well-dressed young lady would wear for any Western class. Note the dark hat and gloves and neat appearance of the neckwear.

This rider's horse has been beautifully groomed and he is well turned out for a Western class.

coordinate yourself with your horse so that you appear as one, not two separate units. If your horse is a sorrel or chestnut, you might choose your color tones in the rust or burgundy family. Is he a bay? Consider chocolate, or a soft shade of brick if he is a blood bay. Match the gold tones of a Palomino or set off the soft shades of a dun with beige. Pick up a shade of gray if his coloring runs to dapples or steeldust. Stick with the grays if your horse is black, otherwise you'll look like Zorro. Whatever choice of color, be *conservative.* Stick to muted tones and no loud patterns, please! Faint vertical stripes or a subtle tattersall are about as wild as you should get. If you are even just slightly heavy, stay away from the light colors like poison. Your weight is going to be more noticeable when you are mounted.

Keep your accessories in the same color family but in a darker shade. This is where a lot of people make an error and choose a lighter hue or even white, which is like putting a neon light on the areas that you want to keep unobtrusive. Reason: your hands and your legs are the aids you use to ride your horse. You don't want the judge to notice when you have to use them. The idea in the ring is to look as if you are a passenger on a machine that has been programmed to follow whatever is required in that particular class. So . . . you visually hide those hands and feet if you are smart. The same thing goes for your head. Don't put a light-colored hat on it. The judge will glance in your direction, see a light-colored object bobbing along, and subconsciously note any rough motion your horse is making. Should you look down to take a peek and see what lead your horse is on or why he has just stumbled, you can bank on the judge's noticing you at that moment.

Chaps

This will be your most expensive item, unless you are fortunate enough to pick up a pair secondhand. Whatever, *don't*

This 4-H rider is a good example of what the well-dressed 4-H'er wears in a show. Her posture is perfect, she has good control over her mount, and she wears a becoming smile.

buy a cheap pair. They will last forever, and if you should want to sell them you will always find a ready market.

The type they are now wearing are called "shotgun" chaps. They are form fitting, with fringe down the side, and they open with a zipper hidden under the length of the fringe. They should be long enough so that they drape over your boot when you are mounted. Be sure to check on what length is popular in your area. In California and certain other Western areas they wear what is termed an "equitation heel." The leather, in this case, is so long that it extends down past the heel of the boot, giving the rider an almost exaggerated "heels-down" appearance. When the rider is dismounted, he must fold the excess leather up so that it won't drag the ground.

As to color, try to get the chaps as close to the color of your horse as possible. Keep them as simple as you can: *no highly contrasting buck stitching* down the side! When you stand this will look nice, but on the horse it will turn into a funny zigzag effect at the knee and negate anything else you do to give yourself that slim, tall-in-the-saddle look. Also, remember to pull your fringe to the back of your leg before you mount or again you are going to get the funny zigzag look because of the way the fringe falls around your knee.

Once you have those expensive chaps, take good care of them. Try to sponge them off with clean water to get rid of sweat stains as well as spot clean them with a good leather cleaner after each wearing. In this way you can avoid having them professionally cleaned more than once a season, and cleaning shortens their life, no matter what they tell you. Store them flat or hang them, but don't fold them.

Boots

Match the color and hue to your chaps. Remember, the idea is to keep the line as long as possible visually. Buy any style or leather of your choice. Just avoid those two-toned affairs, which are best left for square dancing or looking smashing in a halter class.

Equitation Suit

These outfits are the proper attire for girls in most areas of the country. They are truly great. They are easy to ride in and they make the rider look like a million. They should be as form fitting as possible, hence they are usually made of a soft knit material with quite a bit of stretch. They cost a small fortune in the tack shop but can easily be made at home, using a Western shirt and pants pattern. Buy a good stretch material that will hold up under the friction of the saddle and will wash and wear with no ironing. By getting a pattern one size smaller and adjusting it, you should have the perfect fit.

Many people prefer to make these suits into a one-piece jumpsuit affair, but I would advise not. Instead, make the shirt and pants separate and put heavy-duty snaps at the waistline to hold the shirt down. Let me deviate for a moment and explain why.

If you really get into showing, you may find yourself entering your horse in both English and Western classes. Sometimes these are placed back to back, and you have only a few moments to change, certainly not long enough to race to the restroom to do so.

While your friend or relative is doing the honors with the tack change on your horse, you can make this quick change right there at ringside. Let us say you are riding in a Western class first. Wear your English breeches under your chaps with a Western belt over the waistband, and your English choker in place of a tie with your Western shirt. Come out of the class. Unzip your chaps, take off your Western belt, change into your English boots and hunt cap, turn the collar of your Western shirt to the inside and slip the choker to the outside, put on your hunt coat, remount your horse and be one of the first ones into the next class. Reverse the procedure if it is the other way around. Needless to say, you should keep colors in mind when buying, or making, both your English and Western outfits, if you are planning to enter both kinds of competition.

Now back to the Western dress. If you are a more mature woman, or a male, you are not going to be wearing an equitation suit. What you will be wearing is a combination of Western shirt and Levi's or frontier pants along with your chaps. The same visual effect should be striven for, however. Keep the colors as united as possible and stick to a knit material when choosing a shirt so that you will have that body-clinging look.

Hat

The choice of hat and the way it is worn can make or break a rider's appearance in the eyes of the judge. The height of crown and the roll of brim should fit your head and personal stature. And *put your hat on straight.* Wear it so that it fits absolutely level on your head, with the center of the brim roll at the center of your forehead. I have seen a rider who should have placed first in an equitation class put down to fifth because her hat was off center just enough so that she looked slightly out of alignment in the saddle.

As to hair, if you are a girl or woman, you must wear it neatly in a bun at the back of your neck. Cover it with a net and secure it with about a hundred bobby pins. If your hair is so short that you cannot pull it into a bun, buy a false one and secure it firmly. Otherwise you are going to resemble a rather funny-looking boy. Here you can add a touch of silver in the form of a barrette in the center of the bun if that is "in" in your area. This makes a nice present to give or receive, as a good one costs in the neighborhood of $20 or $30.

Accessories

Don't make the error of getting a big, flashy silver buckle for your belt. Better yet, choose one of the belts with a square or oval leather-covered fastener and save the silver for your saddle. The brightness of the polished silver is again going to pull the judge's eye to your waistline, and few people want that.

Gloves are either going to be worn in your area or not. Stick with the group. But if they are worn, why not try a pair of those isometric driving gloves now so popular. They fit your hands better than leather and allow you more freedom of movement as well as being about half the price. And, since most people tend to misplace gloves, you will probably lose them long before they have a chance to wear out. Just don't wear a pair of "dress" gloves. It will ruin your total look.

Your neckwear can be an individual matter, depending upon the area you live in. In some areas the leading choice seems to hold with the standard Western tie, which is tied in a square knot. In some other areas the preference is now turning to the English choker. This is a strip of material, either in a solid color or a bright pattern, cut in a contour so that it lies neatly around the base of the neck under your collar. Only an inch or so shows in front, so pick whatever color or pattern you prefer.

No jewelry, please! Not even those tiny earrings for pierced ears that are so in vogue today. Take them out and leave them out while you are showing. Nothing is tackier than jewelry with equitation gear.

Jackets and Sweaters

Occasionally it gets cold. If you can't afford a good Western-style jacket, buy a heavy cardigan sweater that is not bulky and will coordinate with whatever else you are wearing. Remember, the idea is to stay slim and supple looking, and bulkiness will shoot you down every time. It is better to freeze for fifteen minutes and come away with a ribbon. If warmth is so important to you, stay on the rail and bundle up with a blanket.

HALTER CLASSES

No matter what type of horse you are showing, you will be perfectly proper if you stay with the approved habit for that particular class. But with a Western horse you can go with just a little more color if you want to.

If you can afford it or want to sew up another outfit, you might use the same pattern you used for the equitation suit and make it in a bright material that will complement the color of your horse. Or you can choose one of the lacy Western shirts and coordinate it with a slick pair of plaid frontier pants or Levi's, and those two-toned boots if you want. (No need to wear your chaps in this class.)

The code of neatness still counts, so don't poke a hair brush in your back pocket to spiff up your steed in the ring. That is not the place to do it anyway!

You can even get away without wearing a hat. Sometimes one can be a visual nuisance when you are trying to set up your horse to his best advantage. Keep your hair style neat, though. Braids are rather charming if you can carry them, or pull your hair to the back with a ribbon or silver barrette. You can even throw caution to the wind and buy the biggest and flashiest silver belt buckle you can find.

ENGLISH

Whatever was said about Western attire's being conservative goes double, or triple, for English. Occasionally you will see a girl riding into a class in an electric blue coat or

A good example of a well-fitting saddlesuit worn when riding park or saddle seat. The rider is wearing a soft hat but a derby would serve just as well.

bright green or even purple, and you know that Great Aunt
Matty, bless her heart, made that coat. No self-respecting riding shop has had that hanging on its racks!

What you wear depends on what type of class you will be
showing in most—hunter, jumper, or hunter seat equitation.

Coat

Not too long ago, if you were showing a hunter, you automatically wore the correct hunt attire, which is a black melton coat, yellow vest, stock tie, buff or canary breeches, and
boots with the correct hunting cuff for your sex—black
patent for the lady and tan for the gentleman. But today things
have become a bit less formal and those riding in hunt
classes and jumper classes dress pretty much the same. All
the same, if you are going to attend one of the larger shows
or are going to be involved in the more formal evening
classes or in a specific hunt class where hunt appointments
are required, you should wear the traditional attire as just
described.

If you are going to be involved in local or afternoon shows,
for the most part, you can go with the colors of your choice
as long as they are conservative and coordinate with the
color of your horse.

A hunt coat really looks better in a subtle pattern or
darker shade, as the idea is *not* to match the color of your
breeches. Also a pattern or darker color does not show the
wrinkles as much as a plain or lighter color will, and wrinkles
are bound to occur in hot weather. The popular colors
seem to be brown, olive, medium blue, and burgundy. Most
coats are made either of a wool mixture, lightweight summer
fabric, or double knit. Since the show season falls into both
the warmer and cooler weather, double knits would be the
more suitable. They are cool in summer and correct in winter
and allow you the freedom of movement you need when jumping or just trying to impress the judge.

Ready-made coats are fairly expensive, with a price tag starting in the neighborhood of $75. If you are smart you will get out your sewing machine and make up your own. You need only check through the pattern books for a standard blazer with princess lines, flap pockets in the front, and a deep vent in the back. Buy a good mannish-looking double-knit fabric of medium to heavy weight and stitch up a coat for $12 or $15. As long as you stick to knits and do away with lining, which would negate the give of the fabric anyway, your sewing chores should be easily accomplished.

Breeches

You are going to have to spend a little money here. I doubt that you could or would want to buy these secondhand. But the better ones are made of a material that is cast-iron strong, and unless you really take a tumble they should last you a few years. Buy the best quality you can afford. The standard colors are buff, rust, white, and canary. I personally would avoid buying the white ones. Horse shows are dusty places to say the least, and you can get grimy-looking pretty fast.

There are two prominent leg styles, the no-flare and the slim-flare. If you have great-looking legs, the no-flares will look terrific on you. If, however, you have a problem in the leg area or are a bit heavy, I tactfully suggest you try on the slim-flare to see if they might suit you better. The flare is not like those old horrors in the 1930's movies but is just enough to hide your leg shape, if it is not perfect.

Boots

Because really good boots cost between $100 and $200 and really good boots are what you should have, I would like to suggest you make this a two-step affair.

Let me explain why you really should own a good pair of boots if you intend to do much riding. Your leg is a very important part of your body when riding, and a well-fitting boot will add immensely to your riding performance, safety, and enjoyment. You will wear those boots wherever you ride, not just in the show ring. They'll even go with worn Levi's and a motheaten sweater, and they'll last almost forever. As for looks, picture yourself in an expensive dress or suit and add a pair of cheap shoes. What happens to the total look? Everything looks cheap. The same goes for a pair of ill-fitting boots.

So make your first boot purchase a pair of secondhand ones, which will keep you going for a couple of years until you decide that riding is really for you and you have had time to save up for a pair of custom-made ones.

Besides looking at bulletin boards, be sure to ask the instructors at any riding school. They usually have a back room filled with boots belonging to students who have decided to take up tennis instead. You should be able to find a pair for $20 to $30.

When trying on those boots pay more attention to how they fit on the leg than on the foot. You are not going to be concerned so much with walking as riding. There is nothing as uncomfortable or as dangerous as a too tightly fitting boot; it cuts off the blood supply and you lose the feeling where you need it. And there is nothing that can destroy your total look and scream "amateur" so much as a boot that is too large and does not fit at the top where the breeches meet the boot.

If for some reason you cannot locate a pair of good secondhand ones, you might try a pair of the rubber riding boots used for rainy weather. They are really quite good looking, and if you don't get too close it is difficult to tell if they are rubber or leather. You can buy a pair for around $20.

As for color, stick to either a dark brown or black. If you plan to show in classes where you must wear the regulation hunt attire, you would be better off buying a black pair. You can then buy separate regulation hunt collars to slip over the tops of these and make "instant" hunt boots.

Hat

The standard one worn in all English classes is the "hunt" cap, although if you are ever invited to attend a hunt, or show in a formal hunt class, ladies must wear a derby instead—just one of those whimsical formalities in the horse world. Black is the most worn color, but if your boots are brown buy your hat to match. Avoid such custom colors as blue, green, and burgundy like the plague. Again it gives the feeling that Aunt Matty has been at work in the gift-giving department. Besides, off colors are more expensive. Instead spend that extra money on a hat with a removable safety harness and wear it when you are not showing.

If your hair is long, it should be pulled back in a bun and covered with a hair net. If it is short you may stuff it up under your cap. Just so long as it is neat. When buying your hat try it on with your hair combed the way you will be wearing it; otherwise you may find out too late you have the wrong size; and fit in a hunt cap is all important.

Shirts and Neckwear

Depending upon the section of the country you live in, there are two types of shirts and neckwear now being worn. Be sure to check where your area stands fashionwise before you invest.

Most popular is the "equitation" shirt. This is what used to be called a "ratcatcher" shirt. It has a small standup collar, over which you wear a choker, and it comes in either a long-sleeve or sleeveless style. These shirts are not expensive and if you can afford two, buy one of each. Get them in permanent press and avoid dark colors, which get hot and sometimes "bleed" all over everything.

Color-key your choker to your jacket. They come in a wide variety of colors and patterns, and if you sew you can use your leftover scraps of material to make yourself a wardrobe of chokers. They take about ten minutes to sew up, even by hand. Note: they are great items to make and sell or give as "little" gifts.

The other choice of shirt is that worn by boys and men and in some parts of the country by women. It is simply a long-sleeved dress shirt with standard dress tie. A tie clip or tie tack should be used to keep the tie from flying about.

Vests

This is not a required item unless you are dressed in regulation hunt attire, and then it should be yellow. Frankly, I consider a vest a bit formal and I find it restrictive in jumping and similar activities, but some people always like to dress to the nines; you will find them in every group. Whether you wear a vest or not is strictly up to you.

If you should decide to wear one, go ahead and make it a bright color. In fact, do make it yourself. A vest is an easy garment to sew, and if you are making your own hunt coat you might as well get an extra yard of material and make a vest to match, with a reversible side in a bright pattern or color and a choker to match that.

Accessories

As for gloves, again check to see what they are wearing in your area, and stick with the darker colors if they are "in."

Special belts are nice extras to buy when you want to pamper yourself. They are almost a form of jewelry, resembling laced reins, braided reins, bits and bridles and such. But a plain, everyday one-inch leather belt will do quite nicely.

PARK PLEASURE

In the last several years more and more people have been showing up at the smaller shows with their park pleasure horses, and as a result a somewhat relaxed version of this rather formal type of showing has evolved. However, the attire worn is still best compared to a man's business suit.

Saddlesuit

This should be of a conservative color and well tailored. An ill-fitting saddlesuit looks worse than any other type of garment devised by man. Furthermore, it is hard to find a decent suit for less than $200 or $250.

Hang on! Help is on the way . . . and I'll bet you can guess what it is. You're right, the old sewing machine is involved once again.

This time begin by purchasing a pair of jodhpurs in a standard color for about $35, and then make the jacket yourself, using the same blazer pattern mentioned previously and extend the skirt of the jacket some six or seven inches. Your coat should measure about two inches longer than the tip of your middle finger. Don't forget to line the skirt of the jacket with a waterproof material, as it will be lying across the back of the horse when you are mounted. You should be able to make the jacket for under $20, bringing the total to about $55 for a great-looking suit that will stand up to a $250 one any day.

The most used and most flattering colors seem to be the

browns, beiges, and grays. Blues are quite popular but are hard to match, so be wary of these if you are making your own outfit.

Your jodhpurs should be long. When you are mounted, the cuff should reach the top of your heel. There should be a moderate bell at the bottom. If they are too narrow they will not be graceful and if they are too wide they will twist around and look ungainly. Be sure to fold your cuffs up when you are not mounted to keep them from dragging in the dust.

Boots

There are two types of jodhpur boots: those with elastic sides and those with straps about the ankles. It is a personal preference which style you choose, but the ones with elastic sides are easier to wear and look somewhat more fashionable. The ones with straps do not give as well, tend to bind your ankles when you are riding, and look a bit bulky under your jodhpurs. They come in either tan, brown, or black, and you have merely to decide which color goes best with the suit you are wearing.

Hat

Correctly a hat should be worn with this type of attire, but, as I said, what has evolved is a more relaxed form of saddle-seat attire. Therefore, whether you wear one or not is up to you. In my area it seems to be half and half, with those who feel uncomfortable or feel that they look bad in a hat not wearing one. There are two types of hat that may be worn: the soft snap-brim hat, most favored by boys and men, and the derby, favored by girls and women. It is best to try to match the hat to your suit, but if you cannot find one that matches, go to the nearest neutral color, one or two shades darker than your suit.

Shirt and Neckwear

Nothing hard about it. A regular dress shirt and tie are all that are needed by both sexes.

Vest

If you insist on color, here is the place you should indulge in it. You might want to match the vest to the color of the lining of your jacket or tie. If you do pick up a brighter color accent, it is nice to repeat it with a colored browband for your horse.

Gloves

Since this is such a dressy style of riding you are going to feel rather naked unless you are wearing some. Again, stick to the darker colors.

SMILE!

P.S. It matters not what style of riding you are planning to participate in, the most important accessory is a pleasant smile. Wear one of these and you'll impress the judge and bystanders as well as add to your own feeling of well-being. You'll thereby assure yourself of having a wonderful time . . . and that's what it's all about!

HORSE TALK

Appointments Equipment and clothing used in showing.
Breeches Riding pants that end just below the knee and are worn with knee-length boots. Used when riding the English forward seat.

Buck stitching A form of Western decoration resembling a long running stitch used on saddles, bridles, and leather apparel.

Chaps Originally a seatless overall made of leather and worn by the working cowboy for protection against brush. Decorative ones are worn in Western classes.

Choker A decorative band of material worn about the throat instead of a tie.

Continental length A new shorter length now popular in hunt coats.

Field boot A type of hunt boot that has lacing at the instep. This boot has suddenly gained in popularity in the East, though it has been with us for years. Do not wear it for showing west of the Rockies.

Hunt boots Knee-length boots worn with breeches.

Hunt cap A hard hat lined with sponge rubber and covered with velvet, usually black or brown, meant to protect the rider in case of a spill.

Jodhpur boots Ankle-length boots worn with jodhpurs.

Jodhpurs Long pants worn when riding park seat. There is a variety that is ankle-length and worn by some forward seat riders when hacking. Never wear this type when showing in a forward seat class or when jumping. Boots and breeches are the only correct garb here. Young children are the exception as it is not always possible to fit them with boots and breeches.

Melton A type of material from England used in making hunt coats. Now a term to mean any black hunt coat.

Newmarket boot A hunt boot in which the main body of the boot is made of canvas. Popular with older riders for hacking. Never appear in a show in this type of boot.

Ratcatcher shirt Originally a casual shirt worn for hacking. Now called an "equitation shirt" and worn with a choker for showing.

Saddlesuit Suit worn by those riding park seat. The jacket is long and flaring and the matching jodhpurs have long, belled bottoms. Good tailoring and correct fit are paramount.

Safety harness A removable harness used with a hunt cap when not showing to keep the hat from coming off.

Stock tie A white formal tie worn with proper hunt attire. It resembles a long bandage and was used as such in case of an accident. Traditionally of linen. A large gold safety pin is worn horizontally in the center of the tie and used as a fastener for the bandage.

10

Show Time

ONE FOR the money, two for the show, three to make ready, and four to go. But, before you do, let's be sure you're ready to go and know where you are going.

If you could not care less whether or no the trophies on your shelf bear the letters AHSA, an enjoyable show career can be had right in your own community. You will spend half as much on entry fees, travel half as far to get there, and come home with ribbons and trophies just as handsome as those from a "recognized" show.

On the other hand, if what you want is to do some "serious" showing and you plan to go on to the recognized shows, I cannot overstress the importance of spending one or two seasons on the unrecognized show level first, both to build your confidence and polish your show know-how.

In any case it is these smaller shows that I will be discussing here, and it is at them you will be learning the wheres and hows of showing.

ONE FOR THE MONEY!

Do not be deceived. The smaller shows have come a long way in the last decade. For the most part they are well run, competitive, very professional in makeup, and tend to follow the AHSA rules, which is why they are such an excellent training ground for showing on a higher scale. In almost any section of the country you will find one or more shows scheduled ·for your area each weekend from April through November. By keeping an eye on the bulletin boards of the local stables you will know when the season starts in your particular area. If you attend three or four of these shows first as a spectator—an active spectator—it will help to get you off to a *faux-pas*-free beginning.

Make a game of it. Pick the class or classes you plan to show in a couple of weeks hence and pretend you are actually participating in them at this show. Arrive early and walk through the trailer area as if you had your horse with you. Observe what is happening, where the horses go, how they are unloaded and tied, etc. Then go to the check-in table and eavesdrop to see what is said and how things are done. Now go watch some classes and see if you can pick out the winners.

Try to position yourself near a group that seems to be actively watching the show and do a little more polite eavesdropping. Make a mental note of errors made by the contestants and promise yourself you will not make the same. Check what the riders are wearing and the appointments on the horses. Look for well-groomed horses and riders, as well as those who are badly groomed, and see how they place in the final lineup.

Keep track of when the classes you are "riding" in are due to come up. Go back to the contestants' area and observe them getting ready for "your" class. Pick a rider and put yourself in his or her place—all the way through the class. I promise you this playacting will teach you more in one class than you can learn from several hours of reading about showing. You will even find yourself cheering when "you" win or feeling blue if "you" get the gate.

When lunch break comes take another walk around the grounds and note the things people bring: does everyone bring a picnic lunch or do they buy hot dogs? How casual is the atmosphere? Watch to see how they dress between classes and anything else that might be peculiar to horse-show people in your region of the country.

During the afternoon spend your time watching the judge. Look at the hand movements he makes and see if you can decipher what they mean. See if you can tell how he judges a class. Does he keep the contestants going at one gait for long periods of time or does he make quick decisions? If you do your showing in one geographical area you are probably going to have that same judge at some point during the season, and anything you learn about him now will help you then.

Trivia? Possibly. But knowing the right trivia will help to put you at ease when that big day comes and your stomach feels as if you had suddenly swallowed a bucket of fishing worms.

TWO FOR THE SHOW!

The type of shows offered will depend much upon the area in which you live. If you are deep in the heart of Texas, you will probably see mostly Western classes, with a smattering of English here and there. On the other hand, should you reside in New England or Virginia, the shows will be predominantly English in nature. In California, where I live, the mixture is half and half. At a local one-day show the classes will more than likely be divided, with one type being shown in the morning and one in the afternoon, so that you need only come to the session that interests you.

Posters announcing coming shows will usually have the types of classes offered along with the time and place and name and phone number, or address, of the show secretary, plus information as to whether or not entries must be mailed in or can be made the day of the show. Upon choosing the show that is to be your debut, take down all the information. If the entries are to be mailed in in advance of the show, for

heaven's sake, get one and get it in on time. There is such a thing as a post entry fee if you do not make the deadline.

If you have never been to the place where the show is to be held, it might be a good idea to take a trial run to see what the ring and grounds look like and also to see if you can find your way there with ease. That first trip to a show with your horse rocking the trailer behind you at 6:00 A.M., and with no one in sight to ask directions from, is no time to get yourself lost.

THREE TO MAKE READY!

Are you ready? If you have been practicing daily for the last six or eight weeks you probably are, but ask yourself these questions anyway.

Are you and your steed letter perfect in whatever class you have planned to enter? Does your horse take his leads easily both from a walk and a trot or jog? Is he collected or does he go about the ring with his nose out in front of him and his mouth open? Is he free of any antisocial habits, such as biting and kicking in public? Is your posture show-perfect? Can you use your aids imperceptibly, or are your hands still all over the place and your feet thrashing at your horse's sides? Have you geared your mind so that you can think one move ahead of the person in front of you as well as think of the judge's next command? O.K., now let me discuss those classes you are going to enter.

No matter how confident you now feel about any such activity as jumping or piloting your horse through the maze in a trail horse class, your first show is not the place to present this ability to the world. Stick to something easy the first couple of times.

If you ride Western you might enter a pleasure horse class and/or an equitation class. If you ride English either a pleasure horse or hunter hack along with an equitation class should do it for you. Two classes are just about as much as you should attempt in one day.

FOUR TO GO!

What about those classes you are going to find listed? How do you know what will be expected of you? Well, for starters, let's explore some of the more commonly found classes and what lies therein that you should be aware of.

Western Pleasure Horse Class

At first glance you might consider this to be what it says it is, a class in which a horse proves that he is a pleasure to ride. That would seem a logical type of reasoning. Ah, but no!

In actuality it is more of a beauty contest.

In all fairness it is judged primarily on the smoothness and grace of the horse as he moves along in a relaxed manner, but a flashy hide never hurt an entrant.

This is probably the most overpopulated class in any Western show, and one of the toughest to win. To be in the ribbons your horse has to be not only perfect but *better than perfect.* You will be asked to walk, jog, lope, and back. About eighty percent of all the horses will execute these maneuvers flawlessly. Thus, it will probably be some small thing that will win the class for someone. Here, then, are a few tricks that might help you be that someone.

Be the first one into the class if at all possible. Execute your entrance with a smart, flat-footed walk and as much regal bearing as you can muster. Keep yourself away from other contestants. If you find you are suddenly in a bunch, make a circle and come back to the rail to an empty spot. Do this as quickly as possible; wandering around the center is not the way to attract attention. Try to anticipate the gait the judge is going to call for next and be prepared to go into that gait as soon as it is called.

At the end of the class, when the call comes to line up, stay on the rail long enough (but not *too* long) so that you can be one of the end horses, and then space yourself about two horse widths apart from the nearest horse. This not only helps to place you in the judge's mind but it prevents any possibility that you are going to be caught in between two horses that suddenly take a dislike to one another—a sure way to say good-bye to any possibility of a ribbon.

You will be asked to back individually, after the lineup in the center. Have your horse collected and start your backing just as the judge reaches you, but not before the person next to you has completed his turn. There is nothing a judge hates more than to have to stand there while you get yourself and your horse together—especially if he has walked down a line of about twenty horses. Backing is the downfall of a great

Nice posture for a Stock Seat Class. The rider is composed, looking between the horse's ears, her hands are correctly placed over the horn and she is sitting well into the saddle. Note the "equitation heel" on her chaps, worn in most Western states.

many horses, and if yours does well in this you have a definite advantage.

Do not give up showing at any point during the class. Continue to show even though you think the judge has already done his placing. Sometimes he will fool you and change his mind at the last second—perhaps he had you in mind all along and just wasn't too sure until that other rider relaxed and blew the whole thing. And, if showmanship and sportsmanship mean anything to you, you will continue to show until you have left the ring.

Stock Seat Equitation

To the casual observer there is no difference between the Western pleasure class and the stock seat equitation class. But there is all the difference in the world! In the Western pleasure class it is the horse that is being judged; in the stock seat equitation class it is the rider. But, when the rider is being judged, the horse is also, for it is the rider that must make that horse perform well, and if the horse is not going well, the rider is put down because of it.

Besides the performance of the horse, the class is judged on seat, hands, the appointments of horse and rider, and suitability of mount to rider.

As an entrant in this class you will be asked to perform the same routine as in a Western pleasure class plus possibly being required to dismount and remount, and if there is a tie you may have to change horses with the person you are tied with.

Winning hinges on the way you and your horse perform each movement or *lack of movement.*

Hold your head straight, with your eyes looking forward between the horse's ears at all times, with the exception of your peripheral vision, which should be on the judge. Keep your back straight but not stiff and sit well into the saddle. At

Proper mounting and dismounting in a Western Equitation Class can be the deciding factor in bringing home a ribbon. This is how it is done.

DISMOUNTING

Flip the end of the reins to the near side of your horse.

Put your left hand on the withers and the right on the horn.

With your weight on the withers, not the saddle, dismount, being sure to clear the horse's back.

When your right foot has firmly reached the ground remove your left foot from the stirrup.

MOUNTING

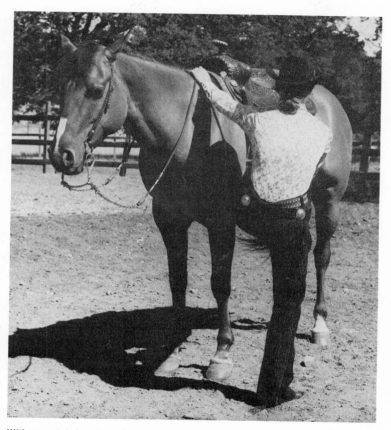

With your left hand on the horse's withers place your left foot in the stirrup while facing the horse's rear end.

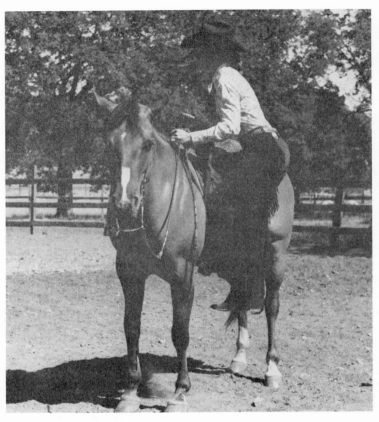

With your weight placed on the withers and your right hand on the horn raise yourself even with the saddle.

Swing your leg over and sit.

Finally, flip the reins to the right side and place your hand loosely on your thigh holding the ends of the reins.

no time lean forward or backward; *no* looking down to see which lead your horse is on. Make all cues and leg movements as subtle as possible; a squeeze should accomplish any change of gait.

The way you hold your reins differs with the type you are using. If they are the *romal* type, make your left hand into a fist, with the thumb pointing upward, and hold the reins so that the quirt end comes through the top of the fist. With your right hand hold the remainder of the quirt, or *romal,* as it comes to the side. Place this hand on your thigh and allow the rest of the *romal* to hang straight down.

If you are using split reins you may place one finger between the reins, with the hand held in the same position as above. Place your right hand on your thigh, resting it casually, with the arm held naturally and close to the body.

To dismount properly, first make a loop of your reins and move this to the near side of your horse, holding all the reins in your left hand. Put your left hand on the horse's neck just in front of the withers and dismount in as smooth a manner as possible. To remount, repeat the procedure. The main point here is the correct timing of the handling of the reins as you mount and dismount—especially if the rawhide reins with the *romal* are used.

If the class is a particularly close one and the judge asks you to exchange horses with another rider, just remember that you are both at a disadvantage. Ride the best you can and carry off whatever happens with aplomb. Perhaps the judge will reward your efforts with a blue.

Trail Horse Class

This Western class is meant to show the ability of the horse to overcome almost any obstacle found on the average trail. Unfortunately, in order to please the public some of these obstacles have become a bit ridiculous. Last year I attended

A typical obstacle found in a Western Trail Horse Class. The rider's attention is on guiding the horse and the horse is responding well.

a large show on the West Coast in which the horse was asked to walk over an elevated plank with a cageful of squawking chickens on one side and a frightened baby elephant on the other. I don't know what trail that show committee had been riding, but I bet it wasn't on a horse!

Some of the standard obstacles you will find are: a gate to be opened, gone through, and closed behind you; a back-through consisting of logs placed in an L-shape; a walkover, which could be anything from a small bridge to a bunch of tires lying on the ground; one or two jumps, such as a small log or imitation stream; and a side pass consisting of a log or pole that the horse is asked to sidestep the length of with his front feet on one side and his back on the other. You may also be asked to put on a slicker or other noisy garment while mounted to test his steadiness.

These hazards are performed individually. The group is then asked to take the rail and is evaluated as a Western pleasure class would be.

If you have a horse with a good, quiet disposition, this is the class to groom him for.

English Pleasure Horse

In the smaller shows this can sometimes be a confusing class. You may find a selection of park pleasure horses going along with hunter hacks. This makes it extremely difficult to judge on the basis of "way of going," for a park pleasure horse should have a much higher degree of collection and action, while the hunter hack is judged almost as one would judge a Western pleasure horse, on ease of action and comfort of ride. All you can hope for is that the judge has his wits about him and can in reality judge two different classes going about the ring at the same time and come up with the proper winners.

Hunter Hack, or Under Saddle

The word "hack" in English riding is meant to describe anything done on the flat by a hunter. This is where those hunter hacks in the last class actually belong, and if you see both types of classes listed at the show, make sure you are not getting in the wrong one.

You will be asked to walk, trot, canter, hand gallop, back, and perhaps negotiate one or two low jumps. It used to be that calls for the canter were always made from the walk, but more and more it is being asked for from the trot. If you have not practiced this with your horse you are going to find him extending the trot before breaking into the canter, and then sometimes picking up the wrong lead. Practice this at home so that he will pick up the correct lead as soon as you give him the signal.

As for the hand gallop, some horses really take off so that it could hardly be considered a controlled gallop. If yours is one of these speed demons, do not just sit there passing horse after horse as if you were in the Preakness. Instead, push him well into the corners or try circling when it is least obtrusive to do so, and when the judge is not looking your way. And don't pull the unpardonable sin of running up someone's tail. That will not only put you well out of the ribbons, it may even get you killed.

If your horse does uncommonly well in one particular gait and you find yourself in an extremely crowded class you might occasionally break the rule that says you should stay on the rail. Take advantage of a bunching and push your horse as if you were going to pass and then take the inside track—*just long enough* to gain the judge's attention—and then back to the rail like a good little rider. After all, when you have that many people to contend with you've got to get that judge's attention somehow.

This rider shows good balance and is alert, as is her horse. The jump is typical of a hunt course.

Hunt Seat Equitation

This is like the stock seat equitation class except that the appointments are English and you are dressed accordingly. The idea is the same, to judge you as a rider who knows how to control his horse and has the proper horse to control. However, there is often one added attraction. Because you are riding a hunter, it is taken for granted you know what to do with a hunter. Thus, occasionally you will be asked to negotiate one or two very low jumps; not over two feet six inches. Therefore, lest this be a surprise to you, practice going over something of this height for a few weeks prior to the show.

Embarrassing situation category: A word about equitation classes. Remember they are to show how well the rider has learned to ride. If you are an adult, the horse world takes it for granted you accomplished that feat early in life and does not look kindly on you if you invade a class meant for those still nursing acne. I remember an incident recently when a lady of silver hair entered such a class. She not only rode badly but she wore the wrong clothes, and when the class had ended she insisted on a blow-by-blow reason from the judge as to why she hadn't placed in the class. I wanted to die for her.

But if you are of the senior group and have recently learned to ride and are proud of that accomplishment, take heart! In recent years a new class has risen on the horizon called the "Jack Benny class," and if you are brave enough to admit to being "over-the-hill" you can go ahead and show the world what you have learned since passing puberty. And if I am anywhere near you I will cheer like mad!

Classes Over Fences

Let us first make sure that we all know and understand the difference between the hunter and the jumper.

The ideal typical hunter is a quiet, well-mannered horse of Thoroughbred breeding or type that has been trained to carry his rider safely and comfortably over the terrain found on an actual fox hunt—even though as a show hunter he may never tread this type of turf.

He is expected to move smoothly, tirelessly, keep up an even pace for long periods of time, remain quiet while the hunt is in check and have good enough manners not to kick another horse or the dogs. He is not expected to have to jump unnaturally high or tricky fences; that is for the jumper.

The jumper can be of any breeding and conformation just as long as he can clear the obstacles placed in front of him with courage and agility. He is not judged on manners or way of going, and no one, with the exception of his rider, cares how smooth a ride he is. Jumper classes are scored mathematically, with points going against the horse on the errors he makes over fences and/or the time it takes him to complete a round.

Jumper classes are the darling of the spectator. They are flashy, fast, and sometimes very dangerous; spectacular falls are not uncommon in the bigger shows. But in the larger shows you will find the jumper classes heavily populated by professionals who expect a fall or two occasionally.

All hunters jump but not all jumpers are hunters. *You cannot have both a hunter and a jumper in one horse.* If you have a lovely Thoroughbred type who moves well and is an enjoyable ride, he belongs in hunter territory. If you have a horse that is spirited, loves to jump, and can make his way over a six-foot gate with nary a switch of his tail, you have the makings of a good jumper and will have an admiring audience every time you enter the ring.

Hunter and Jumper Courses The show hunter course is designed to have some similarity to the cross-country hunt course. The types of jumps will likely include rustic fences, brush jumps to simulate hedges, various kinds of low gates, simulated stone walls, and in-and-outs meant to simulate a lane running between two fences.

The jumper course, in addition to having more spectacular

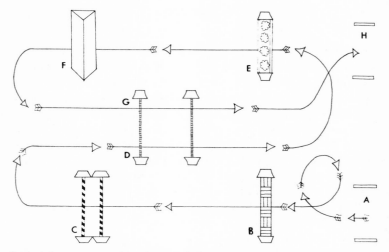

Typical jump course. A, *entrance circle;* B, *brick wall;* C, *double bar;* D, *in-and-out;* E, *brush;* F, *chicken coop;* G, *in-and-out;* H, *exit.*

jumps, is designed to place pressure on the horse and rider, so the jumper must be schooled enough to maneuver quickly and be able to change his stride easily to accommodate tight spaces. Black and white striped poles placed on standards of varying heights, sloping panels painted in wild designs, treacherously high gates, simulated brick walls, and triple in-and-outs are some of the mental hazards to be found awaiting the riders in this class.

In addition to types of jumps, there is one further difference between hunter and jumper fences. The hunter fence is equipped with wings, or side panels, while the jumper fence is not. This is because a hunter is not expected to just jolly well jump anything in his path. He has to have a reason, and his jump is considered to be over a fence, or wall, or similar object.

Riding the Course Upon arriving at the show, one of the first things to do is memorize the course you will be riding. This will be posted near the in-gate. If the course has already been set up in the ring and you are not interfering with anyone, you might walk it on foot, getting a mental picture of how many strides it is between jumps and how wide you will have to swing on the turns. And, if yours is not the first class, you might watch some of the other horses take the course so that you can make any changes in your strategy. Perhaps there is a soft spot or wet spot that has bad footing. Sometimes there will be one particular jump that no horse seems to like and all will refuse, or hesitate at it. If you are aware of these problems before your turn you will be prepared.

When your class comes up, be ready but don't stand clumped with the others at the in-gate. Keep your horse walking so that his muscles are warmed up when he enters the ring. Upon hearing your number called, make your "entrance circle" with your eyes already over that first jump. If you are mentally already over that first one you are off to a good start. Sit quietly and keep your horse moving at as smooth a pace as possible. Judge your approaches so that you won't be making any "proppy" jumps—those in which the horse has been allowed to take off too close to the jump. Even seasoned riders have trouble keeping their form and balance over a proppy jump; and there is little time between that jump and the next to regain your balance and a possibly lost stirrup.

If you get a refusal, do not make a large production of it. Sometimes it is easier to back your horse four or five steps and have another go at the jump rather than make a large circle and give him time to think about another stalemate. And, should you be tooted out of the ring for having too many refusals, *exit promptly,* nodding politely to the judge and refraining from taking out your feelings on your horse. Do not waste the judge's time, the steward's time, and the spectators' time by making the show ring a schooling ring. Chances are your horse will keep on refusing and you are going to feel like a bit of an idiot. Letting your horse get away with not jumping that one particular jump is not going to ruin him . . . honest!

Hunter Classes

Hunters are classified in two ways: by size and experience. Classes are arranged according to these classifications and combinations of classifications. For instance, you might enter your horse in a Junior (age of the rider) Lightweight (size of the horse) Handy Hunter (experience of the horse) Limit (number of ribbons won by the horse in that division) class.

In the large hunter shows it is possible to find enough variety of classes to fill a good-sized two-day program, but in the smaller shows these classifications are clumped together into broader categories. Below are some of the more common classifications.

- Lightweight Hunter. Capable of carrying up to 165 pounds.
- Middleweight Hunter. Capable of carrying up to 185 pounds.
- Heavyweight Hunter. Capable of carrying over 185 pounds.
- Maiden Class. Open to horses that have not won a first in the division in which they are being shown.
- Novice Class. Open to horses that have not won three firsts in the division in which they are being shown.
- Limit Class. Open to horses that have not won six firsts in the division in which they are being shown.
- Green Hunter Class. Open to horses that have not been hunted for more than one season and that have not won a first in the Hunter Division before January 1 of the current year, except in classes requiring no performance over jumps exceeding three feet six inches.
- Qualified Hunter Class. Open to horses that have been regularly hunted with a recognized pack.

- Working Hunter Class. Open to all hunters, qualified or not.
- Handy Hunter Class. Rather like the Western trail horse class, in that it is supposed to demonstrate the hunter's abilities on the open trail. The jumps are of the type found on a more difficult cross-country course. Also the rider may be asked to open and close a gate, dismount and lead his horse over a low jump, etc.
- Hunter Hack. As mentioned previously, this is actually a class on the flat, but it is included here as you may be asked to negotiate a couple of low jumps, depending upon what the show committee has decided would make an interesting class.
- Conformation Hunter. Any class in which the conformation counts more than 40 percent.

Jumper Classes

The following classes are to be judged on performance *alone.*

- Maiden Jumper Class. Open to horses that have not won a first in the division in which they are being shown.
- Novice Jumper Class. Open to horses that have not won three firsts in the division in which they are being shown.
- Limit Class. Open to horses that have not won six firsts in the division in which they are being shown.
- Open Jumper Class. Open to all jumpers.
- Touch and Out Class. Winners are decided by the most obstacles cleared without a touch. Horses are excused as soon as a touch is made.

This is a good example of showing at halter in a small show. The girl showing the Appaloosa is well out of the way of the judge and has her horse at attention. The girl in the background still is keeping her eye on the judge even though he has finished with her.

- Knock Down and Out Class. Winners are decided by the most obstacles cleared without a knockdown. Touches do not count. The horse is excused as soon as a knockdown occurs.
- Scurry Jumpers Class. Class is judged on time, with one second being added for each fault instead of the usual scoring. The winner is the one whose score is lowest in seconds.

Halter Classes

You and you alone know if your horse is worthy of showing at halter. The size and nature of the show determines whether or not you will feel comfortable putting your lovable but slightly cow-hocked Matilda through her paces.

The halter class is a beauty contest—nothing more, nothing less. In addition to having outstanding conformation, your horse must be in the peak of health and groomed to perfection. He is to be shown at a walk and trot and stand for inspection.

The walk and trot are performed individually in front of the judge. He will tell you to take one gait to a distance away from him, turn and come back on the other gait. Your horse must travel willingly, with you moving along near his shoulder. After all the horses have gone through this procedure you will line up and await the judge's inspection. When the horse stands for the lineup he must immediately square up. To square up means that his legs should be standing squarely underneath him. If they are too close together it will make him appear humpbacked; if they are too spread out he will look swaybacked.

After he is standing the way you want him, you are to move in front of him, holding the lead loosely in one hand. Your horse must be willing to stand there some twenty to thirty minutes, all the while looking alert.

There are several tricks used to achieve this state of alertness. Some trainers keep popping the lead strap; at home they flicked the horse's nose with it and he remembers this quite well. Others use some sort of noise-making device, such as a couple of pieces of sandpaper glued to their thumb and index finger and rubbed together, or possibly a small metal cricket, which they click when the judge is not near, or there is that ever-popular jangling-of-the-keys-in-the-pocket routine. Whatever it is, try to avoid doing it while the judge is near you.

When the judge approaches you, be sure to keep an eye on his movements and *do not get between him and your horse!* Move so that you are always facing him, even if it means switching the lead from hand to hand and moving yourself around considerably.

Do not lose your alertness either—you never know when the judge is going to glance in your direction to compare some point on your horse with the one he is judging at that moment.

Finally, do not despair should you fail to place in the ribbons. Even though the class is to be judged on a standard conformation ideal, the judge may prefer another type of horse over yours and award him the blue even when "everyone" recognized it "belonged" to you. Take yourself on to next Saturday's show. Perhaps the judge there will prefer your type of horse.

P.S. A WORD ABOUT JUDGES

Judges *are* human . . . no matter what you've heard. For the most part they are intelligent and knowledgeable men and women who have gallantly given of their time, usually for very little money, to stand in a hot arena for some eight to twelve hours trying objectively to find the best horse in each class. So don't berate a judge for a decision until you have tried

Youngsters with ponies can enjoy the fun of small backyard shows. This 4-H'er is running the barrels in a Gymkhana Class.

performing this duty yourself. Take whatever decision was made and accept it with a sportsmanlike attitude. Next time it may be someone else grumbling about *your* beating *him* out. After all—that's show biz!

HORSE TALK

AHSA show A show recognized by the American Horse Show Association.

AQHA show A show recognized by the American Quarter Horse Association.

Check-in table Area where you check in when you have arrived at the show area. You are given your number, or numbers, at that time. One number for each horse you are riding.

Entrance circle The circle you make, after entering the ring in a fence class, to establish the correct lead.

Get the gate To be excused from the ring.

In-gate The entrance to the show ring. It may be the same gate as the exit, but still called the in-gate at the beginning of the class.

Inside track The track area away from the rail, usually taken in order to pass someone.

On the rail To ride next to the rail.

Out-gate The exit from the show ring.

Post entry fee A penalty paid for not getting your entry in on time. Does not apply at shows where entry fee is paid at check-in time.

Ring steward Person (may be more than one) in charge of the ring. Also assistant to the judge at some shows.

Show committee A group of people responsible for the details of putting the show together. Those to whom legitimate complaints are to be made.

Show secretary Person responsible for compiling lists of entrants and accepting entry fees.

Ticks A jump nicked by either the front or rear legs of the horse.

Wings The extension or side panels of a jump used in a hunter class.

11

Why Didn't
Somebody Tell
Me That?

AND NOW for a potpourri of information—some important, some not so important—tidbits that may put you one up at the next gathering of the horsy set, or possibly may save your life or your horse's someday if you are aware of them.

There is no particular order (I think it's more fun that way) so you may dip in wherever you choose. There are even a couple of blank pages at the end for you to add your own bits of gossip.

* * *

If you want to make your horse feel good, scratch his withers. Most horses are really pretty lukewarm about your patting their faces, but scratch their withers and they are in heaven.

* * *

Ever wonder why horses hate the dark? Perhaps it is because their natural enemies count on the dark to do their meal procuring.

* * *

Horses are a gregarious lot, and they have an inborn need for leadership. It is these two qualities that allow man to dominate the horse. He looks to you for friendship *and* leadership. *Do not fail him!*

* * *

Your horse's emotional state often shows in the way he holds his tail. When he is happy and it is a four-star day for him, he will carry it high and proudly. When he is unhappy and mulling over whether or not to give the next interloper a swift kick, he tucks his tail tightly against his buttocks.

* * *

There is an old saying that wall-eyed horses are mean. This is a lot of nonsense. It merely means that there is a lack of pigment in the iris.

* * *

The eye of the horse has an irregular-shaped retina. Instead of focusing as we do, he moves his head around until he finds the image he is looking for.

* * *

A horse quickly learns to respond to simple word commands, such as "yes" and "no," as long as they are consistently used to have the same connotation.

* * *

When leading a horse give a series of little tugs. All he needs to know is that you want him to follow you. If you give a steady pull, he thinks you want him to pull back. This is one reason why people sometimes have trouble loading their horses into trailers.

* * *

Horses are one-sided. A horse's brain is in two parts and he can't put the knowledge from one side into the other and vice versa. So if you teach him something on one side you will have to repeat the lesson again on the other side.

* * *

The sweat glands of the horse are located mainly in the neck area, back, shoulders, and groin. There are no sweat glands on his limbs.

* * *

Because of his eye positioning, the horse's usual view is to either side; only with concentrated effort does he focus his eyes to a forward view. But, if he is grazing with his head down, he can pretty much see what is going on all around him. Funny how nature planned it this way, since the horse in the wilds spends much of his time grazing.

* * *

Did you ever wonder why horses snort so much of the time and how they do it so well? They have a false nostril, which they fill with air and then expel it with wondrous noise. I have a feeling that some horses think this is quite nifty and do it for a lark—at least whenever I have on a clean white shirt.

* * *

Watch your horse sometime as he carefully picks his way through a rocky area. Rarely will his back feet stumble, yet he cannot see them. What makes this possible is his proprioceptive sense. A small center in his inner ear sends messages to his brain and allows him to retain an accurate picture of exactly where each forefoot landed so that he knows where to put his back ones. Nice planning, huh?

* * *

A horse kicks for two reasons. Either he is frightened and trying to protect himself or *he has been spoiled* (not by you, I trust).

* * *

Most horses suffer from astigmatism and see things in a rather distorted manner.

* * *

The average horse's head weighs about twenty-four pounds. When placed on his long neck it then becomes a ballast which is used like a pendulum to maintain his balance when running and jumping.

* * *

Few horses are leaders, or want to be. Most prefer to stay safely inside the pack. What makes a horse race, then, if no one wants to be leader? Perhaps it is only the natural "escape reaction" that makes horses run when others do—to escape some form of danger. Think about that the next time you enjoy a race. You may be watching a group of frightened horses that believe they are running for their lives.

* * *

Radiation is perceptible to horses and they will not venture anywhere near material that contains uranium ores. Do they know something we don't?

* * *

When you consider it, a horse that jumps is pretty marvelous. In order for him even to see the jump he must keep his head up or he loses sight of it in either a blind spot or a blurred one. Furthermore, when he gets to within four feet of the jump he can no longer see it at all. The next time your horse refuses a jump, put yourself in his place and I'll bet you won't be so ready to berate him.

* * *

Do not despair if your horse appears to be a slow learner. Latent learning is quite common in the equine world. You may spend a frustrating hour trying to teach your steed to do something, throw up your hands and walk away, only to find that the next time you see him he will perform instantly.

* * *

If a traumatic experience is associated with an object or place a horse will retain the memory of that object, or place, for years. And it need not be a specific place or object either—merely similar. If he was hurt going over a particular type of bridge, you can rely on his having a dislike from then on for all bridges even slightly resembling the offending one.

* * *

Horses are color blind, or at the most they see very limited color. They view the landscape as a series of mosaics and depend on shades and brightness to find such things as water to drink and grass to eat.

* * *

Never accuse your horse of not having an active imagination. When he spots something moving unexpectedly, he is probably conjuring up all kinds of horrors that will do him harm. So the next time your horse jumps four feet straight in the air when a facial tissue blows across the road, don't call him stupid. To him it might be a horse-eating tiger.

* * *

An acute sense of hearing is one of your horse's best assets, and loud noises bother him. He prefers either a high-pitched sound or a whisper. Try whispering sweet commands in your horse's ear and see if he isn't a better horse for it.

* * *

There is a theory that the color of a horse has an effect on its mental makeup. Black horses are said to have edgy personalities and tend to rear; chestnuts are flighty and hot tempered; grays are quiet and dependable; while bays are stubborn and arrogant. You may take this with a block of salt or file it away for future reference.

* * *

Index

References to illustrations are given in *italic type*.

Notes

Notes

Notes